The Literacy Approach to Teaching Foreign Languages

Ana Halbach

The Literacy Approach to Teaching Foreign Languages

Ana Halbach
Department of Modern Languages
University of Alcalá
Alcalá de Henares, Madrid, Spain

ISBN 978-3-030-94878-8   ISBN 978-3-030-94879-5 (eBook)
https://doi.org/10.1007/978-3-030-94879-5

© The Editor(s) (if applicable) and The Author(s), under exclusive licence to Springer Nature Switzerland AG 2022
This work is subject to copyright. All rights are solely and exclusively licensed by the Publisher, whether the whole or part of the material is concerned, specifically the rights of translation, reprinting, reuse of illustrations, recitation, broadcasting, reproduction on microfilms or in any other physical way, and transmission or information storage and retrieval, electronic adaptation, computer software, or by similar or dissimilar methodology now known or hereafter developed.
The use of general descriptive names, registered names, trademarks, service marks, etc. in this publication does not imply, even in the absence of a specific statement, that such names are exempt from the relevant protective laws and regulations and therefore free for general use.
The publisher, the authors and the editors are safe to assume that the advice and information in this book are believed to be true and accurate at the date of publication. Neither the publisher nor the authors or the editors give a warranty, expressed or implied, with respect to the material contained herein or for any errors or omissions that may have been made. The publisher remains neutral with regard to jurisdictional claims in published maps and institutional affiliations.

This Palgrave Macmillan imprint is published by the registered company Springer Nature Switzerland AG.
The registered company address is: Gewerbestrasse 11, 6330 Cham, Switzerland

To all teachers who take risks and explore new ways of teaching to help students develop to the best of their abilities.

Foreword

Foreign language teaching has undergone a thorough overhaul in the past decades. The shift to communicative methodologies took place nearly 40 years ago and an onus on "communicating to learn" (Halbach, this book) approaches like CLIL (Content and Language Integrated Learning) has dominated the foreign language teaching scene for over two decades in our context. CLIL implementation has also evolved in exciting new directions. From a more reductive approach which tended to dissociate the communicative and conceptual continua and to evaluate language and content separately, we have veered towards a more integrative stance which conflates academic and disciplinary literacy (Pérez Cañado, 2020) while concomitantly favoring a systemic-functional view of evaluation (Otto, 2018), both in line with a pluriliteracies approach (Meyer et al., 2015) which develops cognitive discourse functions (Dalton-Puffer, 2013).

However, language competence outcomes are still not up to scratch in Spain, despite these efforts to align language teaching methodologies with more significant, meaningful, and deeper learning approaches. Indeed, according to the *English Proficiency Index* (Education First, 2019), Spain still occupies one of the bottom rungs on the foreign language knowledge ladder in Europe, and the *Cambridge Monitor* study (Cambridge University Press, 2017) likewise confirms that our country has one of the lowest English levels in the European Union. Why are we still miserably failing to reach the desired standards despite attempts to reconfigure our language learning panorama? The answer to this question undoubtedly lies in the literacy approach on which this book expounds, which could well be the lynchpin to turn the aforementioned situation around and to transition successfully towards truly communicative, memorable, and content-informed language teaching.

In this sense, the present volume constitutes a genuine personal and professional step change on the foreign language teaching scene. It presents a novel approach which is fully aligned with the latest trends in the field (student-centeredness, trans-disciplinarity, pluriliteracies, multimodality, twenty-first-century soft skills), but which goes above and beyond prior proposals by applying the aforementioned concepts concretely and seamlessly to grassroots practice. It thereby offers an important rejoinder to the well-documented rift between theory and on-the-ground classroom praxis that still unfortunately pervades in language education scenarios. In this sense, it shakes up current CLIL implementation by setting forth an innovative proposal to foreign language teaching which is distinctive on three counts: by laying out an updated and well-crafted definition of literacy, by characterizing a novel pedagogical approach, and by offering clear-cut recommendations for its practical application.

Indeed, the book departs from a *new conception of literacy*, which transcends the more narrow, traditionally upheld view which associates it to the ability to read and write. Instead, it focuses on identifying content which is specific to language teaching, integrates focus on form in its just mean, and ties in with student-centeredness, learning strategies, and key twenty-first-century soft skills which allow students to navigate critically and skilfully the vast amount of information they have at their disposal. Literacy is also defined in the classroom context, with a distinction being drawn between basic, intermediate, and disciplinary literacy. In the initial section itself, the book crafts a compelling case for the urgent need to develop this type of literacy in present-day teaching, thereby showcasing the clear niche which the proposal comes to fill.

The latter is then addressed via the *innovative pedagogical approach* it unfolds. Text types are used as the organizing principle of foreign language teaching at all educational levels, in both the L1 and the FL/L2, in order to favor two-way transfer between languages. This approach allows a natural integration of skills, a meaningful contextualization of language work, and memorable, significant learning. It also orchestrates a much-needed balance between seemingly contradictory dichotomies such as focus on input versus output or meaning-based versus form-focused instruction.

The final step further narrows down the level of concretion by presenting the *practical application* of the literacy approach. This section walks the reader down the learning path with the help of a very illustrative planning grid, displays, videos, or checklists which clearly evince that the teaching sequence herein proposed is not just wishful thinking but tried, tested, and successful. This is also beautifully illustrated via the real teacher and student comments with which the book is peppered. The proposal is ground-breaking in favoring a backward design which starts by identifying the final result (students' production), defines learning goals and standards, and only then proceeds to the selection of contents, tasks, and materials. The two phases of the learning path (reception and production) are aptly broken down, presenting them from the students' perspective and sustained with carefully selected scaffolding, attuned to each phase. Students are encouraged to move from what the text says to what and how it means, fostering critical reading and making the process understandable, enjoyable, purposeful, and engaging. The teacher, in turn, is freed from the shackles of the textbook and encouraged to unleash his/her creative flair in designing original unit plans where language comes directly from the text and no longer needs to follow a pre-established order. Assessment of students' production also acquires a sharp relief in the practical application of the proposal: it is formative, feedback-focused, and diversified (through self- and peer evaluation) and fosters student awareness of what has been learned.

Further guidance is furnished to take this approach to the grassroots level by offering a practical example of a literacy unit for primary education, by explicitly signposting how to make it compatible with the existing language curriculum, by identifying the chief difficulties inherent in its implementation, and by providing teacher training directions to empower practitioners to step up to it. And this is always imbued with a great sense of realism and practicality, acknowledging that, as with any pedagogical innovation initiative, a success-prone implementation of the literacy approach requires time to take root and teachers should start small and then scale up its implementation.

As the bard and oracle Bob Dylan signaled, "The times, they are a-changin'." And the present proposal is a sine qua non to spark that change. It is high time we realigned foreign language teaching with the true needs of twenty-first-century society; we took pluriliteracies, multimodality, and trans-disciplinarity to new heights by truly applying them to grassroots practice; and we transitioned successfully to communicative, meaningful, and content-informed language teaching. This much-needed change is precisely what the literacy approach brings about. This trailblazing proposal creates an invaluable lens through which to approximate foreign language teaching and reshape our encrusted educational structures. If you've wondered what we were previously missing to ensure our language levels are up to par and to unlock the full potential of language teaching in our immediate context, this is it. Informed by the latest trends, stemming from a rich and prolific experience and reflection, and fueled by the always far-reaching vision of the author, this proposal is a tour de force for anyone interested in taking the quantum leap in foreign language teaching.

Universidad de Jaén   María Luisa Pérez Cañado
Jaén, Spain
November 2021

References

Cambridge University Press. (2017). *Cambridge Monitor 4. Europa ante el espejo*. https://www.cambridge.es/nosotros/cambridge-monitor/europa-ante-el-espejo

Dalton-Puffer, C. (2013). A construct of cognitive discourse functions for conceptualising content-language integration in CLIL and multilingual education. *European Journal of Applied Linguistics, 1*(2), 216–253.

Education First. (2019). *Education first: English proficiency index 2019*. https://www.ef.com.es/assetscdn/WIBIwq6RdJvcD9bc8RMd/cefcom-epi-site/reports/2021/ef-epi-2021-spanish.pdf

Meyer, O., Coyle, D., Halbach, A. Schuck. K., & Ting, T. (2015). A pluriliteracies approach to content and language integrated learning-mapping learner progressions in knowledge construction and meaning making. *Language, Culture and Curriculum, 28*(1), 41–57.

Otto, A. (2018). Assessing language in CLIL: A review of the literature towards a functional model. *Latin American Journal of Content & Language Integrated Learning, 11*(2), 308–325.

Pérez Cañado, M. L. (2020). What's hot and what's not on the current CLIL research agenda: Weeding out the non-issues from the real issues. A response to Bruton (2019). *Applied Linguistics Review*. https://doi.org/10.1515/applirev-2020-0033

Acknowledgement

This book is the result of many years of work as a teacher and teacher trainer. The approach described here developed slowly—like all good things—and with the constant input of language teachers in primary and secondary schools mainly in Madrid (Spain) but also in Poland and Slovenia. Without their questions, suggestions and experience in putting the approach into practice, it would never have reached this stage. In particular, I would like to thank Marta, Irene and Marta for being brave enough to embark with me on the Erasmus+ project and change their approach to teaching. My big thanks also go to Kasia and Mateja for inviting me to join them in a project of this kind, as well as to Elena and Raquel, my loyal project partners at Alcalá.

Very special thanks to Marisa for accepting to write the foreword even though she had enough on her plate already and to my daughter Sara, who was crucial in tidying up the visuals for the book. I am also grateful to my editor Cathy Scott, who did a good job convincing me that I could, indeed, write a book!

Lastly, I need to mention the two persons whose part in this project is beyond measure. Eva, the first believer, and my firm link to real-life classrooms. It has been a privilege to see what happens in the classroom when literacy becomes the focus of teaching through her eyes. And without Daniel, my husband and partner in this and all adventures in life for the past 25 years, none of this would have been possible. From our very first ideas about how to change language teaching as part of the preparation of a shared teacher training course to the endless revisions of this book, thank you, thank you, thank you!

Contents

1	**Communicating to Learn: Giving Language Teaching a Content of Its Own**	1
	Why Literacy Development?	3
	What Does Literacy Development Offer to Foreign Language Teaching?	6
	Outlook	9
	References	9
2	**The Literacy Approach**	13
	Planning	13
	Backward Design	14
	Students' Final Production: Text Types and Modes	15
	The Teaching Points	19
	The Learning Path	19
	The Planning Grid	23
	Outlook	27
	References	28
3	**Designing the Learning Path: The Reception Phase**	29
	Starting with the Text	29
	Leading Students into the Text	30
	Understanding and Enjoying the Text	31
	Looking at How the Text Means	33

Putting on the Writers' Glasses: Observing *the Text*   33
Working on the Language: Analysing *the Text*   36
Organizing the Learning Path with the Help of the Planning Grid   37
    Outlook   44
References   44

4 Designing the Learning Path: The Production Phase   45
Ready for Production   45
Giving Students the Opportunity to Focus   46
What Guided Production *Looks Like*   47
Time for Free Production   50
Guiding Students Through the Free Production *Stage*   51
Assessing Students' Production   57
Outlook   59
References   59

5 A Literacy Unit in Primary Education   61
Becoming Clear About What We Want to Teach   61
From What I Know to What I Could Not Do Alone—The Learning Path   63
Outlook   72
References   72

6 Integrating a Literacy Approach Into an Existing Curriculum   73
But I Have a Curriculum to Follow …   73
A Whole School Approach to Literacy Development   78
Developing an English Curriculum That Feeds into the Content Subjects   82
Language Teaching as Part of Students' Academic Development   86
Outlook   88
References   88

7	Teachers and the Literacy Approach	89
	Just Take Any Step, Whether Small or Large ...	89
	Training the Teachers	93
	Why Literacy, Why Now?	95
	References	96

**Appendix A: Tasks for the Reception Phase of a Unit Based on
We Were Liars by E. Lockhart** 97

**Appendix B: Checklist of Contents for Year 10 in the
Curriculum of Advanced English (Comunidad de Madrid,
Spain)** 101

Index 107

List of Figures

Fig. 1.1	Types of literacies according to Shanahan and Shanahan (2008, p. 44)	5
Fig. 2.1	The planning process in backward design	15
Fig. 2.2	The learning path	20
Fig. 2.3	The teaching sequence in the Literacy Approach	21
Fig. 3.1	Graphic organizer for explanations, adapted from Brisk (2015, p. 252)	35
Fig. 3.2	Reception stage in the unit based on "Comment ça marche la voix?"	41
Fig. 4.1	Structure bank	48
Fig. 4.2	Worksheet: making a text more informative	49
Fig. 4.3	Description of a fantasy dog	52
Fig. 4.4	Display reminding students of the purpose and characteristics of a biography	53
Fig. 4.5	The process of writing	55
Fig. 4.6	Self-assessment checklist	58
Fig. 6.1	Poem about witches in Spanish	81
Fig. 6.2	Poem about vampires in English	82
Fig. 6.3	Rhyming recipe for a magic potion in French	83

List of Tables

Table 1.1	Comparison of a traditional approach with the Literacy Approach to foreign language teaching	8
Table 2.1	Characteristic features of different text genres (adapted from Brisk, 2015; Derewianka & Jones, 2016)	16
Table 2.2	The first part of the planning grid	24
Table 2.3	Extract from the first page of the planning grid for a unit on *The Gruffalo*	25
Table 2.4	Extract from the first page of the planning grid for a unit on *The Gruffalo* including a description of the level of performance expected	27
Table 3.1	Second part of the planning grid (blank)	39
Table 3.2	Excerpt from planning grid for the reception phase for "Comment ça marche la voix?"	42
Table 5.1	First part of the planning grid for a unit on instructions (Spanish)	62
Table 5.2	Second part of the planning grid for a unit on instructions (Spanish)	65
Table 6.1	Items from the curriculum for Advanced English (year 10) for bilingual schools in the Comunidad de Madrid, Spain (Madrid, 2018), covered in the reception phase of the unit on *We Were Liars*	75
Table 6.2	Distribution of genres across the six years of primary education including the three languages in the curriculum	80
Table 6.3	Extract from the syllabus for Advanced English, year 8, description	85

CHAPTER 1

Communicating to Learn: Giving Language Teaching a Content of Its Own

Abstract This chapter situates the approach proposed in the book against the backdrop of current moves in language teaching towards "communicating to learn" approaches, away from the focus on "learning to communicate" (Waters, *System*, 53(3), 141–147, 2015). It argues that "communicating to learn" approaches have often failed to transition into the language classroom because they lack a specific content that is to be communicated about. In the approach proposed, this content is identified as the development of literacy. Literacy development lies at the heart of the Literacy Approach described in the book, and the chapter provides a first overview of the approach.

> *If you go to England, for example, you'll not ask for a meal in a restaurant in writing, but you will order orally. I think it's more important to know how to speak English well rather than knowing the grammar. (Tenth grade student)*

Many of the students we interviewed for a research project in 2019 and 2020 made comments about the lack of relevance of what they were learning in their English lessons for their lives. And true enough, despite starting to learn a foreign language at a young age, students' foreign language levels have not necessarily increased, and many of them opt out of learning foreign languages at the first opportunity possible (Devlin, 2018; Long et al., 2020).

© The Author(s), under exclusive license to Springer Nature Switzerland AG 2022
A. Halbach, *The Literacy Approach to Teaching Foreign Languages*,
https://doi.org/10.1007/978-3-030-94879-5_1

Language teachers, meanwhile, experience the frustration of teaching a foreign language, often having to repeat the same explanations over and over again without seeing any result. Despite the fact that the communicative approach has dominated foreign language teaching for almost 40 years now, students in formal education settings often leave school without being able to truly use the language for communication (Eurostat, 2020). Something is going terribly wrong in the field of foreign language teaching, but what is it and how can we turn this situation around?

The truth is that, despite the communicative outlook embraced by most foreign language curricula all over the world, the driving force behind these curricula, what articulates them, is still the grammatical structure, carefully sequenced by difficulty (Mickan, 2013). The idea is that we need to learn the grammar first to then be able to communicate by using it, but as Peter Mickan (2017, p. 21) aptly said, "[i]t is an irony that pedagogies dismantle texts, reduce discourse to a list of grammatical items and words extracted from texts, only for learners to have to learn how to reassemble the objects as texts for participation in communication."

To redress this situation and assure that foreign languages are learned effectively, the past 20 years have seen—at least in academia—the rise of approaches to teaching foreign languages that try to create a need to communicate, in order for students to actually use the foreign language rather than focus on learning it without an immediate need to use it (Waters, 2012). In this kind of approach, the role of the elements of the language—grammar, vocabulary and pronunciation—becomes more incidental and comes as a response to the students' communicative need rather than acting as the structuring principle for the curriculum (Larsen-Freeman, 2003). Most prominent among these "communicating to learn" approaches (Waters, 2015) are Task Based Language Teaching (TBLT), Content and Language Integrated Learning (CLIL) and Content Based Instruction (CBI). However, while prevalent in the theoretical discussions in the field of foreign language teaching, most of these approaches have not readily translated into real classroom practice, as pointed out by Waters (2012). The author suggests that the reason for this divergence between theoretical thinking and actual classroom practice may lie in situational constraints such as students' expectations, their learning preferences and stakeholders' beliefs, etc. (Ur, 2011). Even though these contextual forces have a clear limiting influence on foreign language teaching, or any kind of teaching for that matter, it is also true that there is at least one "communicating to learn" approach that has gained wide acceptance over the past years: CLIL.

While it is in itself problematic to classify CLIL as an approach to language teaching, centred as it is on content subject teaching in a foreign language (Coyle et al., 2010), the fact that it is content-driven is perhaps what makes it different from the rest of the approaches grouped under the label of "communicating to learn" by Waters. Maybe the reason why the other approaches have less successfully transitioned into actual classroom practice lies precisely in the lack of a clear content for language teaching. The fact that the focus of the "communicating to learn" approaches lies on communication immediately begs the question about the content of this communication: what will students communicate about? The concept of *task* around which teaching is organized in TBLT is rather vague and has no clear focus in terms of content, while the content of CBI coincides with that of the content subjects alongside which it is taught. For foreign language teachers following a CBI approach this may turn into a problem, as the contents of the non-linguistic subjects, especially as we move up in secondary education, become increasingly specialized and therefore may be beyond the language teacher's reach. Too specialized a content may not be the answer, but, conversely, without a clear content, an approach focused on communication will not succeed.

Rather than identifying this content with a focus on grammar, linguistic functions or lexis—the study of language—as in the more traditional "learning to communicate" approaches, I suggest that what is necessary is to find a content that (1) is particular to language teaching and (2) naturally integrates a certain degree of focus on form. At the same time, this content should be compatible with all the other elements that the profession claims to be necessary in present-day foreign language teaching: learner-centredness, a focus on learning strategies and a contribution to the development of twenty-first century skills, among which critical thinking, information literacy, reasoning and argumentation and creativity feature large (Pellegrino & Hilton, 2012). This content, as will be explained in the following paragraphs, is "literacy".

Why Literacy Development?

Literacy is often, quite reductively, understood as the ability to read and write (David et al., 2000). However, over the past 20 years or so the term has widened its meaning to "acquiring, creating, connecting and communicating meaning in a wide variety of contexts" (Government of Alberta, 2009). The development of appropriate literacy skills has become more widely recognized as the incorporation into a literate culture that makes it possible for children to develop the secondary discourses necessary for being successful in

> interaction[s] with people with whom one is either not 'intimate', with whom one cannot assume lots of shared knowledge and experience, or [which] involve interactions where one is being 'formal', that is, taking on an identity that transcends the family or primary socializing group. (Gee, 2015, p. 175)

Literacy also helps us navigate the *knowledge society* that is characterized by the wide availability of knowledge that, in principle, would make it possible for every individual to further his or her education, thus creating equal chances for everybody (UNESCO, 2005). However, to be successful in using this enormous amount of knowledge, it takes more than simply being able to understand a spoken or written text. A successful member of society has to be able to interact critically with the wealth of information provided, be able to distinguish what is reliable from what is not, put order into different kinds of information from different perspectives, and generally extract that information which is both meaningful and likely to further his or her understanding and lifelong learning (Directorate-General for Education, Youth, Sport and Culture, 2012).

However, for learning to be effective, it is not enough to simply *receive* information and organize it, but it is also important to communicate it, and do so in a skilful way. Neil Mercer and his colleagues (2004) suggest that teaching children to use certain linguistic structures in talking about their learning improves this acquisition of knowledge and understanding (see also Pellegrino & Hilton, 2012). Knowledge is better understood if talked about, and talking about the knowledge helps both understanding and developing the necessary literacy skills (Meyer et al., 2015), since, as we know from Vygotsky's research, "human reasoning is essentially dialogic, and so functions best when set in argumentative contexts" (Mercer, 2016). Thus, the more we engage students in precise articulation of thinking and understanding, the more they will refine this understanding and at the same time become increasingly skilled in using precisely the literacy skills they need to access information in the first place.

In the context of schooling, literacy takes different shapes. Apart from the classifiers attached to the general noun "literacy" (digital literacy, critical literacy, etc.), we can also identify different levels of complexity,

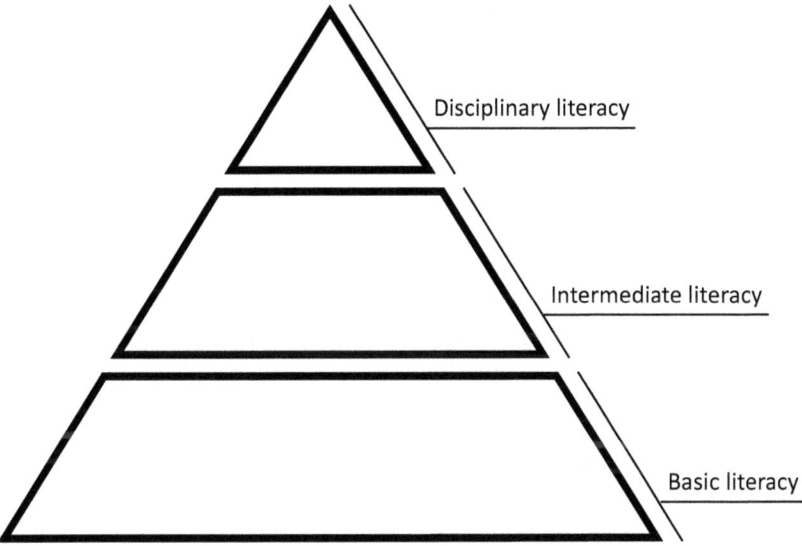

Fig. 1.1 Types of literacies according to Shanahan and Shanahan (2008, p. 44)

distinguishing between *early* or *basic literacy*, concerned mostly with the mechanics of reading and writing, and *advanced* or *intermediate literacy*, which involves higher levels of engagement with texts and whose development starts around the third grade of primary education (Goldman, 2012). Shanahan and Shanahan (2008) add to this distinction a further level of literacy: *disciplinary literacy* (Fig. 1.1), which refers to the literacy practices that are specific to the disciplines (history, geography, etc.).

What is interesting in Shanahan and Shanahan's vision is that this pyramidal representation implies that one level of literacy is based firmly on the previous, so that in order to reach the highest level of literacy development, *disciplinary literacy*, the student has to have developed a sound foundation in both *basic* and *intermediate literacy*. The authors point out that progression from *basic* to *intermediate*, and even less from *intermediate* to *disciplinary*, literacy will not happen spontaneously. And yet, while the pyramid shown "illustrates the increasing specialization of reading skills […] a similar structure could be used to accurately illustrate the declining amount of instructional support and assistance that is usually provided to students as they progress through the grades" (Shanahan & Shanahan, 2008, pp. 45–46). It seems, therefore, that literacy development is an urgency for today's teaching in general but also one that is often not responded to (see also Gibbons, 2002).

What Does Literacy Development Offer to Foreign Language Teaching?

Literacy—literature—grammar translation. This may be a quick association in more than one mind in the context of foreign language teaching, conjuring images of students sweating over obscure literary texts as models of language. However, while literary texts do play a role in the approach to literacy that is proposed here, the focus is on students understanding, enjoying and producing texts of different types in different modes (visual, written, spoken, audio-visual), while becoming increasingly aware of the specific characteristics of the different text types and modes as well as of the power of language. The work is characteristically organized around text types, or genres, such as descriptions, narratives, etc. recounts (Llinares et al., 2012; Martin & Rose, 2015), expressed in different modes. Traces of this kind of approach to teaching based on text genres can be found in the language arts curricula in some countries such as Germany. It has also been used in some contexts, mainly Australia, New Zealand and Singapore, with second language (L2) students but has only marginally become known or used in other parts of the world or in the context of teaching a foreign language. Where it has been used in this context, it is often for advanced language courses at college level (Paesani & Allen, 2012). However, I would like to argue here that there is no reason for not using text types as the organizing principle of foreign language teaching at all levels, especially in formal education contexts, where literacy development will probably also be the focus of first language (L1) teaching. Working on text types in both the L1 and the foreign language (FL), or the L2, has the advantage that students can transfer what they have learnt about the structure and conventions of these genres in their mother tongue to the foreign language, and vice versa, thus linking the new learning to understandings they have already developed.

At the same time, making text the organizing principle in foreign language teaching allows for a natural integration of skills work. Rather than having to work on the communicative skills in isolation or through topic- or task-based, somewhat contrived, contexts, in literacy-driven language teaching reading leads naturally into writing, and listening into speaking, since the texts read and listened to act as models for students' own production. At the same time, if room is created for interaction in class, speaking and listening, drafting and re-reading, and all the rest of the skills and sub-skills will naturally become part of the same learning process. We do not need to *do reading exercises* or *practise intensive listening* since all these skills will be integrated purposefully in a natural way.

This skills integration, and the fact that there is an overarching guiding principle, also allows for meaningful contextualization of language work, both of a formal and of a functional nature. Different genres or text types typically require different language functions which, in turn, are realized by various grammatical structures. Likewise, different text types on various topics will require different kinds of lexis which will be built around a common semantic field. As promoted in the Lexical Approach, the fact that lexis is learnt and used in a context will also foster work with language chunks, or combinations of words typically used together, rather than vocabulary items in isolation. The same contextualized, and therefore meaningful, learning will become possible in relation to pronunciation, with correct intonation and pronunciation becoming a tool for successful literacy practice rather than an end in itself. Literacy-based teaching requires direct instruction of language, but language that is contextualized and purpose-oriented, thus overcoming the seeming dichotomy between meaning-based and form-focused instruction (Waters, 2015).

It could be argued that all these benefits already accrue in current language teaching, much of which is based around an oral or written text for comprehension as well as various production exercises dealing with the topic of the text and the corresponding language elements. However, if we look more closely, we often find that the texts read or listened to have been created to illustrate the use of a given grammatical structure or a number of vocabulary items the unit focuses on. These grammatical structures and vocabulary items are often also the focus of the exercises that form the rest of the unit, with the production exercises mostly coming at the end of the unit and offering students little support and guidance to be able to deal with them successfully.

The approach that is being proposed here is different in that the starting point of the planning process is the expected student output, with the rest of the steps in the unit being directed towards the successful production of this output—hence its learner-centredness. These steps involve

Table 1.1 Comparison of a traditional approach with the Literacy Approach to foreign language teaching

Traditional approach	Literacy Approach
Planning starts from grammatical structure/semantic field	Planning starts from text type (oral or written) that students have to produce
Texts written to illustrate use of a grammatical structure	Authentic/simplified texts
Works on four communicative skills	Integration of four skills: texts are read or listened to, talked about and responded to in speaking or writing
Works at sentence level	Works at text level
Language as object of study	Language as tool for communication
Works on grammatical structures in isolation	Studies language in the context of a text: meaningful and sustainable learning
Aim of teaching unit is to master a certain type of vocabulary/grammatical structure/language function	Aim of unit is to produce a given text type with specific characteristics
Oral and written production comes at the end of the unit and is not guided or supported	Whole unit is designed to make oral or written production successful
Own programme and sequencing	Works towards the language needs of students in the content subjects taught in an FL

both text comprehension and analysis of the textual features, and they work on the language typical of a given text type and topic. At the same time, the reading or listening texts used are not pedagogic texts written to showcase certain language features but rather texts produced for a native-speaker public. In Table 1.1, the differences between a traditional approach to language teaching and the Literacy Approach are summarized.

What Table 1.1 tries to capture is an approach in which all the work done in a unit is contextualized and leads to a final production by the students which is guided and scaffolded in such a way that they can be successful. This makes the learning memorable and meaningful: students use what they learn about the language for their own communication—oral, written, visual or audio-visual—and they perceive this difference:

> We had never learnt like this. No teacher before taught the way she taught us. [...] For me, I think we can say that this was the best unit that we have [ever done]. [...] We would like this method to expand to other schools because we loved it. (Sixth grade students talking about a literacy unit taught when they were in their fourth year)

Outlook

The approach presented here is not fundamentally different from other approaches using texts, from Communicative Language Teaching to Text-Based Teaching or a Genre-Based Approach. What it does, though, is integrate what can be considered best practice from many of these approaches by providing a clear context for the language dealt with, including form-focused work that moves beyond the level of sentence, focusing on students' needs and making learning standards and expected outcomes explicit. It also manages to overcome some of the dichotomies often established in the profession such as a focus on input (Krashen, 1998) versus a focus on output (Swain & Lapkin, 1995), the opposition between genre-based pedagogy and process writing (Hyland, 2010) or that between a focus on form and meaning-based teaching (Waters, 2015). As is recognized by most scholars in the field, the individual teacher, more often than not, uses an eclectic approach to language teaching, and the model presented, in a way, gives shape to this eclecticism.

In the following chapters the approach to teaching foreign languages through literacy—the Literacy Approach—will be described in detail, always with a reference to what it looks like in practice. The examples taken come mostly from English language teaching, because this is the context I, and the teachers I collaborate with, work in, but since the principles are general and applicable to all languages, the approach can be used for teaching any foreign language.

References

Coyle, D., Hood, P., & Marsh, D. (2010). *CLIL: Content and language integrated learning*. Cambridge University Press.

David, T., Raban, B., Ure, C., Goouch, K., Jago, M., & Barriere, I. (2000). *Making sense of early literacy. A practitioner's perspective*. Trentham Books.

Devlin, K. (2018). *Most European students are learning a foreign language in school while Americans lag*. https://www.pewresearch.org/fact-tank/2018/08/06/most-european-students-are-learning-a-foreign-language-in-school-while-americans-lag/

Directorate-General for Education, Youth, Sport and Culture (2012). *EU high level group of experts on literacy. Final Report*. Luxembourg: Publications Office. http://dx.publications.europa.eu/10.2766/34582

Eurostat. (2020). *Foreign language learning statistics*. https://ec.europa.eu/eurostat/statistics-explained/index.php?title=Foreign_language_learning_statistics

Gee, J. (2015). *Social linguistics and literacies: Ideology in discourse* (5th ed.). Routledge.
Gibbons, P. (2002). *Scaffolding language, scaffolding learning.* Heinemann.
Goldman, S. R. (2012). Adolescent literacy: Learning and understanding content. *The Future of Children, 22*(2), 86–116.
Government of Alberta. (2009). *Living literacy: A literacy framework for Alberta's next generation economy.* Alberta Advanced Education and Technology. https://deslibris.ca/ID/220887
Hyland, K. (2010). *Second language writing.* Cambridge University Press.
Krashen, S. (1998). Comprehensible output? *System, 26*(2), 175–182. https://doi.org/10.1016/S0346-251X(98)00002-5
Larsen-Freeman, D. (2003). *Teaching language: From grammar to grammaring.* Heinle.
Llinares, A., Morton, T., & Whittaker, R. (2012). *The roles of language in CLIL.* Cambridge University Press.
Long, R., Shadi, D., & Loft, P. (2020). *Language teaching in schools (England).* House of Commons.
Martin, J. R., & Rose, D. (2015). Genres and texts: Living in the real world. *Indonesian Journal of Systemic Functional Linguistics, 1*(1), 1–21.
Mercer, N. (2016). Education and the social brain: Linking language, thinking, teaching and learning. *Éducation & Didactique, 10*(2), 9–23. https://doi.org/10.4000/educationdidactique.2523
Mercer, N., Dawes, L., Wegerif, R., & Sams, C. (2004). Reasoning as a scientist: Ways of helping children to use language to learn science. *British Educational Research Journal, 30*(3), 359–377. https://doi.org/10.1080/01411920410001689689
Meyer, O., Coyle, D., Halbach, A., Schuck, K., & Ting, T. (2015). A pluriliteracies approach to content and language integrated learning—Mapping learner progressions in knowledge construction and meaning-making. *Language, Culture, and Curriculum, 28*(1), 41–57. https://doi.org/10.1080/07908318.2014.1000924
Mickan, P. (2013). *Language curriculum design and socialization.* Multilingual Matters.
Mickan, P. (2017). Text-based research and teaching. In P. Mickan & E. Lopez (Eds.), *Text-based research and teaching* (pp. 15–35). Palgrave Macmillan.
Paesani, K., & Allen, H. W. (2012). Beyond the language-content divide: Research on advanced foreign language instruction at the postsecondary level. *Foreign Language Annals, 45*(1), 54–75. https://doi.org/10.1111/j.1944-9720.2012.01179.x
Pellegrino, J. W., & Hilton, M. L. (2012). *Education for life and work.* National Academies Press. https://doi.org/10.17226/13398.; https://www.nap.edu/catalog/13398/education-for-life-and-work-developing-transferable-knowledge-and-skills

Shanahan, T., & Shanahan, C. (2008). Teaching disciplinary literacy to adolescents: Rethinking content-area literacy. *Harvard Educational Review, 78*(1), 40–59. https://doi.org/10.17763/haer.78.1.v62444321p602101

Swain, M., & Lapkin, S. (1995). Problems in output and the cognitive processes they generate: A step towards second language learning. *Applied Linguistics, 16*(3), 371–391. https://doi.org/10.1093/applin/16.3.371

UNESCO. (2005). *Towards knowledge societies.* http://www.unesco.org/new/en/communication-and-information/resources/publications-and-communication-materials/publications/full-list/towards-knowledge-societies-unesco-world-report/

Ur, P. (2011). Grammar teaching: Research, theory and practice. In E. Hinkel (Ed.), *Handbook of research in second language teaching and learning* (Vol. 2, pp. 507–522). Routledge.

Waters, A. (2012). Trends and issues in ELT methods and methodology. *ELT Journal, 66*(4), 440–449. https://doi.org/10.1093/elt/ccs038

Waters, A. (2015). Cognitive architecture and the learning of language knowledge. *System, 53*(3), 141–147. https://doi.org/10.1016/j.system.2015.07.004

CHAPTER 2

The Literacy Approach

Abstract In this chapter, the rationale for the Literacy Approach is explained, looking at the way units of work are planned starting from the back, by identifying the expected outcome of the unit. As we move through the process of planning, some key concepts in the approach such as text, teaching point and learning path will be explained.

> *Learning about backward planning has made me switch the way I plan and organise units of work. By being aware of what I want students to produce as a final outcome and what our final learning goals are, I am now able to break down all the tasks in order to make sure that content is properly scaffolded. (Violeta, primary school teacher and MA student)*

Planning

As teachers, our planning normally starts from the contents we want (or have) to teach. Based on the mandatory curriculum, we distribute the contents over the weeks or the terms of the course and then decide what we are going to teach when. We then think about how to teach these contents, i.e. what activities we are going to use and what materials we will need. At least this is the theory, because in practice—at least in my country, Spain—this task is often done for us by the textbook writers, so the textbook we use acts as the syllabus. But even here, when we open the textbook, the first thing we find are the lists of contents and skills that are going to be taught.

However, in real life we don't plan that way. When I plan my holidays, I think of the kind of holidays I would like, whether I want to get to know a new country or rather prefer to spend a week relaxing on the beach. When I plan my husband's birthday party, I start from an idea of what this party should be like, some kind of image of this party. Only then, when I have "dreamt up" the final event, do I start thinking about what I need to do, what food I am going to prepare or who I am going to invite. First the dream, the complete picture, then the steps to reach it!

Backward Design

This way of planning, starting from the end, is generally known as *backward design* (Wiggins & McTighe, 2005). In backward design, rather than starting from the identification of contents and procedures, planning moves through three different steps:

1. identification of the final result of the unit of work, or the question "What should students come away understanding [or being able to do]?" (Wiggins & McTighe, 2005, p. 47);
2. definition of learning goals and standards that we want students to achieve, or the question "What will count as evidence of that understanding [or ability]?" (ibid.) and
3. selection of contents, teaching tasks and materials, or the question "What texts, activities and methods will best enable such result" (ibid.).

The starting point of the planning process therefore is the end of the teaching sequence: the students' production—very much in the same way as my planning of a party starts with a vision of the party, i.e. the result of my preparations. Once I have a clear idea of what I want my students to achieve or be able to do, I need to ask myself what this production looks like, or what constitutes a satisfactory production—what does my party look like in terms of food, guests, setting, etc. This step allows me to formulate clear expectations for students' work and at the same time gives me, as the teacher, a clear idea of what I need to teach my students if I want them to be successful in their production. Finally, I will need to think about the tasks and materials that will help the students develop the necessary skills and understandings for a successful production. Figure 2.1 gives you a visual representation of this process of planning

Fig. 2.1 The planning process in backward design

Students' Final Production: Text Types and Modes

As we said in Chap. 1, the Literacy Approach organizes the work around different text types (recipes, stories, explanations, descriptions, etc.) in different modes (visual, audio-visual, written or spoken), so that the end product we are working towards in each of the units of work is a specific type of text. This sounds very complicated, and surely beyond the reach of primary school children, but in actual fact can be as simple or as complex as we want it to be. For example, the text I might want my young learners to produce can be three sentences describing a monster that they have drawn (Halbach, 2018), while for my upper secondary students it could be a commentary of a design of their choice in a fashion show. The type of text is the same, a description, but the level of complexity varies greatly, as does the mode (written and audio-visual).

Texts take all sorts of shapes, and, in the words of Peter Mickan (2017), "our normal experience of language is as text." From a WhatsApp message to a formal speech, any stretch of meaningful language is some kind of text, but not all texts are the same, as depending on their purpose they will be structured in a different way, include different elements and use language that is typical for it. These different text types are often referred to as genres, and authors working in the tradition of Systemic Functional Linguistics (Martin & Rose, 2012) have long been analysing and classifying these text types. Table 2.1 summarizes the differences between these different genres looking at their purpose—or what they are used for—providing examples of this genre and analysing their organization (stages of the text) and the language features that normally appear in them. For example, if we look at one specific text type, in the "chronicles" genre you will find biographies and autobiographies as one of the types of chronicles

Table 2.1 Characteristic features of different text genres (adapted from Brisk, 2015; Derewianka & Jones, 2016)

	Purpose	Genre	Types of text (examples)	Stages of the text	Language features
Engaging	To entertain	Stories	Narratives Anecdotes Fables Personal Recounts	Introduction of character & setting Complication (resolution)	Verbs in past tense Temporal links Narrative strategies to create tension
Informing	To tell what happened	Chronicles	Historical recounts (recount of a historical event) Biographies and autobiographies	Orientation/context/background Record of stages Evaluation/comment (optional)	Temporal linkers Adverbs, prepositional phrases, conjunctions Verbs in past tense Ends with an evaluation of importance of event, often going from specific to generic participant
	To provide information about a general class of things; to organize information	Reports	Descriptive report (description of an animal, e.g.) Classifying report (description of different types of transport)	General statement Feature 1 Feature 2 Feature 3	Technical terms Generic participants Timeless verbs in the present tense Verbs of states, relations
	To explain how things work or why they happen	Explanations	Historical explanations (examine cause and consequences) Science explanations (why and how scientific phenomena occur)	Phenomenon Explanation Phenomenon Explanation	Cause consequence organized logically Evaluative language Clause structure to express importance Verbs of action, state or relation Generic (abstract) participants Verbs in present tense Nominalization (for logical sequence) Passive voice
	To give instructions or report on a procedure	Procedure	Recipes Instructions for doing an experiment Instructions Procedural recount	Purpose Equipment Steps Result (optional)	Action verbs Imperatives Person is not named Markers of sequence in time Specificity through the use of adjectival, adverbial and prepositional phrases

Evaluating	To evaluate or interpret a text/film	Criticism	Personal response Review Interpretation (commentary)	Context/Synopsis of text/plot Analysis Evaluation	Verbs of action and state to summarize text/film Verbs of sensing to express effect of the text Complex noun groups Sequence and location markers Evaluative adjectives Verbs/phrases of opinion + recommendation
	To argue/persuade	Arguments/ expositions	Argument Essay/presentation defending one point of view Discussion Essay/presentation explaining two+ opposing points of view	Thesis Issue and background information Arguments: point and elaboration Resolution	Sensing verbs (consider, believe, like) Relating verbs (result, symbolize) Generalized participant Complex noun groups Nominalization (idea or event is represented by noun group)

frequently used in school. This text type is characterized by using the following structure:

1. Orientation/context/background
2. Record of stages
3. Evaluation/comment (optional)

Some of the language features that are typical for biographies are expressions of temporal linkers, the use of verbs in the past tense and, in the evaluation, a general noun describing the group of people the person being described represents or belongs to. Knowing about these features helps the students be aware of some of the characteristics of the text they will have to produce. However, it also helps them understand texts of this kind, as this awareness of the features of the text type acts as a kind of guide through the written text, video or speech. And it also helps us as teachers to know what we need to be working on in a unit on biographies and what we need to be looking for in students' productions, i.e. what makes a text a good biography. This last point also helps us identify good model texts to work on with our students.

The specific form texts take is also determined by a second factor, the mode in which this text is presented. The rough distinction that comes to mind between spoken and written language needs to be further refined, as many of our written modes, e.g., WhatsApp messages, include elements from spoken language (contractions, sentence fragments, etc.) as well as features that are particular to this mode, such as abbreviations. This means that a written biography prepared for class may have the same structure as a video presenting the biography of a famous person, but there will also be features that differ, if only because the use of images adds further dimensions and effects to the meaning. Therefore, when we think about a text type we want to work on with our students, we also need to think of the mode in which it is going to be produced: will I ask my students to produce a narrative in the form of an email message or will it be an audio recording of a story in which sounds and dialogues can be included and pronunciation and intonation become important? Depending on my answer to this question, I will have to focus my teaching on some aspects or others, while still working with the same structure and language features. And, also depending on this answer, I will look for an appropriate input text that will act as a model for students' own production.

What we are doing by thinking of text types and modes in this way is what in backward planning constitutes the second step, defining goals and standards for students' production. When I am aware of what constitutes a good text, I am able to define these learning goals and standards, and they determine what it is I am going to focus my teaching on, the teaching points.

The Teaching Points

The teaching points of a literacy unit are directly derived from the features of the specific text type I am going to focus on, as shown in Table 2.1, but will also come from the particular characteristics of the text chosen as input. For example, I could choose to work with my students on narratives and decide to use *The Gruffalo* (Donaldson & Scheffler, 2012), a well-known children's story most teachers—at least of English—will be familiar with, as a model text. This would allow me to include *rhyme* and *pronunciation* as a teaching point in my unit plan, not because it is typical of narratives but because this particular text offers me this feature.

However, we can't focus on all the features a given text offers, or we will bore our students to death. We have to be selective. The focus will have to be on those elements that are within the reach of the students—not too basic and not too difficult—and that directly contribute to the quality of the text they have to produce. We will probably go over each of the text types several times over the years, and therefore what has not been dealt with the first time the students worked on a given text type can be the focus of their work the second time round. This, of course, requires a great deal of transparency in the planning as well as communication among teachers in the process of planning.

As mentioned earlier, the teaching points we select for work in a particular unit constitute the "contents" of the unit, so that the process of identifying these teaching points situates us in the second step in the backward planning model. In the third step, we need to focus on the activities and materials that will help us make sure that all students in our classes are able to successfully produce the text we are focusing on. In a way, what we have done up to here is look at where we want our students to get and, taking into account what they are able to do right now, what they need to learn to get there. How this learning is organized and what shape it takes by means of various tasks and activities constitute the learning path that students will follow in order to reach the final goal, their production.

The Learning Path

When I plan my holidays, I have a clear goal in mind, and by imagining the holiday, I identify what features will make it successful. Knowing this now allows me to plan the steps I need to take to prepare the holiday: choose a destination, convince the family that this is indeed the holiday we all want, book flights and accommodation, arrange for somebody to look after the dog or water the plants and finally pack the suitcases. These different actions all have a different moment in time when they need to be done, and all together constitute a path to a successful holiday.

My teaching plan is similar to planning these holidays: I plan a series of steps that will make it possible for my students to produce the chosen text type successfully, and there are steps that need to be taken a long time before the students start producing and others that come immediately before their production—just like packing my suitcase will hardly be the first step I take when planning my holiday. This constitutes the learning path (Fig. 2.2) that will lead students to be able to create successful texts.

To help teachers structure this learning path, the teaching sequence has been divided into two different phases, reception and production, and each of these is further divided into various steps, as can be seen in Fig. 2.3.

As can be seen in Fig. 2.3 the learning path always starts with a model text that students first understand and enjoy. This is important, as the model text constitutes an example of successful communication. If its main purpose for communication is not fulfilled, we are stripping the text of its primary reason to exist, and it becomes a simple model of language without communicative intent—a random combination of words and sentences with the purpose of teaching the language. In fact, because the texts chosen are good models of skilful communication, they are likely to

Fig. 2.2 The learning path

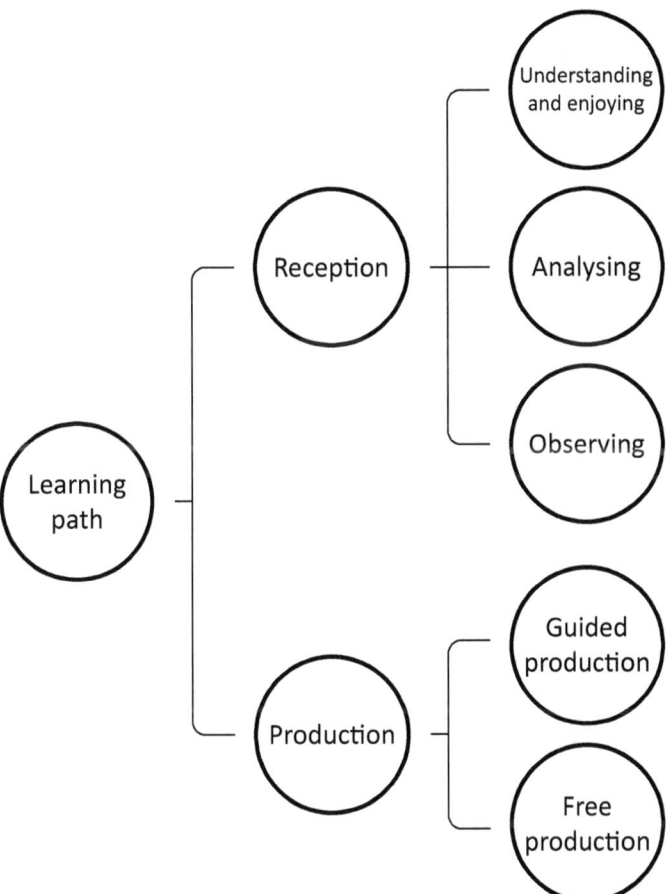

Fig. 2.3 The teaching sequence in the Literacy Approach

trigger a response from students, leading to discussions, questioning or criticism in a way pedagogic texts normally cannot.

> *The texts selected to create the units motivated arguments very often such as the topic of hunting in The Magic Finger, spoiled children in Charlie and the Chocolate Factory or cruelty in farms in Fantastic Mr Fox. Others, such as Letter to my future self, caused a deep reflection on the present and the future stimulating students' interest in knowing about what their peers thought. (Eva, primary teacher)*

The next two steps, *observing* and *analysing*, focus on the way the text is structured and achieves to communicate (*observing*) as well as on the language functions, vocabulary or pronunciation features that are relevant and interesting in this particular text (*analysing*). The reason this has been divided into two different steps is that when texts are "exploited" in language classrooms, this is often done with a view to showing how a certain grammatical structure or a series of vocabulary items are used. Very rarely do we look at how the ideas are organized, how the speaker draws us into a story or how the writer makes us perceive a text as factual and therefore reliable. This is the perspective taken in the *observing* phase, and in a way it leads on to the *analysing* stage, since the strategies the writer or speaker uses to create an effect are realized by certain phrases and language structures or through the choice of certain words rather than others. The two phases of *observing* and *analysing*, therefore, will often be linked in the actual work on the text, but in order to make sure that *observing* does not get lost on the way, it is left as a separate step.

The text that serves as an input for the unit is then used as a model for students' own production. However, even after having understood how the text they have to produce works, students will need to be able to experiment and get to grips with its features before they can be expected to use them in their own production. This is the aim of the *guided production* phase, which thus serves as a preparation for the final output.

This progression through the different phases in the unit (see Fig. 2.3) makes the learning path coherent, since all the tasks centre around the input text, using it first as a text to be enjoyed, understood and analysed and then as a model for students' own production. All the tasks are further planned to lead to students' success, and students therefore perceive them as meaningful and relevant to their learning. They don't study a certain grammatical item because this is what the syllabus says but because this is a structure they will use in their production. Students identify how a text is structured because they will use this structure in their own texts and therefore they need this understanding. Finally, students practise certain aspects of the text because this will allow them to use these features in their own production and thus creates the necessary conditions for them to become successful communicators.

> *For me, working with this literacy approach has been very important. I come from a very traditional way of learning languages and for many years I have been teaching that way where the grammar and the study of language were the*

main issues, and then the production was taken for granted. But in the end, we saw that that was not always true, so discovering literacy has been really helpful and it has been an impulse to my career. I've seen that by this approach children are more engaged, they are really motivated, they suddenly see the purpose of what you are doing and without realizing they are learning, they are learning much more, and in the end the production of the children does really happen, and is really really much better than what we used to have before. (Marta, secondary teacher, over 25 years of experience)

THE PLANNING GRID

To make it easier for teachers to plan their units, in the course of an Erasmus+ project that focused on literacy teaching (see https://lit4clil.uw.edu.pl/ for more information), we created a planning grid consisting of two parts. The first one (Table 2.2) focuses on identifying the main aim (text type) we want to work on and the teaching points the model text chosen offers. It also establishes the levels we expect our students to achieve. This corresponds to the first two steps in backward planning: defining a final aim and identifying the goals and standards we are looking for in this final production.

The second part of the planning grid, which is going to be the focus of the next two chapters, lays out the learning path (Table 3.1 in Chap. 3) and divides the planning into the two phases that were described above: *reception* and *production*. It then develops their corresponding steps of *understanding*, *observing* and *analysing* in the reception stage and *guided production* and *free production* in the production stage. Although this looks like a static and rather rigid sequence of tasks, the Literacy Approach asks for much greater flexibility and iterativity than can be represented on paper. It is true that the learning path always starts with understanding and enjoying the model text, but the observation of the text can already be partly integrated in this step of understanding and enjoying and will certainly be linked in part to the analysing step.

If we think, again, about the children's story *The Gruffalo*, the author skilfully creates interest by having the mouse describe an imaginary monster—the Gruffalo—little by little, focusing on different physical characteristics and always using a structure of adjective + noun ("knobbly knees", "turned-out toes") further characterized by alliterations through the repetition of sounds ("**k**nobbly **k**nees", "**t**urned-out **t**oes"). In this case, then, by *observing* the text, readers will notice that the picture we get of

Table 2.2 The first part of the planning grid

Unit overview

Unit:	Text type (narrative, factual description, procedure....) :	Text selected
Date:		Written/oral/visual:
Level/age:		Author:
		Available at:
	= General aim of the unit	

Teaching points – specific aims (as relevant)

		Teaching point								Level expected
Textual	Text features (organization of ideas; narrator; use of direct speech; paragraphing; etc.)									
	Text effect (creating tension; vividness of descriptions; objectivity; coherence; etc.)									
Linguistic	Language functions / structures									
	Vocabulary									
	Pronunciation									
	Academic language features									
Cultural										
Strategic (learning and thinking strategies)										
Cross-curricular links										
Emotional skills										
Development of values										

the Gruffalo is completed as we progress through the story up to the point where the monster finally appears and that the descriptions made of it are appealing and vivid. Further analysis, in the *analysing* stage, will allow the students to realize how these descriptions are structured, what kind of vocabulary is used and how sounds are played with. The focus thus shifts from the "text effect" to the language used to create this effect and probably back to the text effect to look at other interesting features the text has to offer (see Table 2.3).

Table 2.3 Extract from the first page of the planning grid for a unit on *The Gruffalo*

		Teaching point
Textual	Text features (organization of ideas; narrator; use of direct speech; paragraphing; etc.)	Tension through partial description
	Text effect (creating tension; vividness of descriptions; objectivity; coherence; etc.)	Vivid descriptions
Linguistic	Language functions / structures	Adjective + noun
	Vocabulary	Suggestive adjectives ←
	Pronunciation	Alliteration ←
	Academic language features	
Cultural		
Strategic (learning and thinking strategies)		
Cross-curricular links		
Emotional skills		
Development of values		

We have not, so far, looked at the last column in this first part of the planning grid, the one specifying the level expected. Continuing with the same example from *The Gruffalo*, let's imagine I am going to work with my students on vivid descriptions, as the text I am going to ask them to produce is a description of a monster of their own creation. I would now have to think about what I can reasonably expect my students to produce and describe this as closely as possible in the "level expected" column. In this case, students are expected to become aware of the effect of withholding information, they should be able to place the adjective correctly in front of the noun to describe at least four features of the monster, use three interesting adjectives—beyond "big" and using colour adjectives—and create at least one alliteration (see Table 2.4). This level should describe what I expect all students in the group to be able to do in their production, or what awareness, strategy use, etc. I am expecting them to develop. It describes the minimum learning I am expecting, and experience shows that beyond that, students' work will often stretch beyond the teacher's dreams, as learners are motivated to try out new things, become adventurous in trying to use the language productively and to show all they know.

Look at my description! Isn't it great? (Fourth year primary school student)

By establishing a horizon of expectations in this way, teachers know exactly what they have to work towards, what will constitute a good production and how students' learning will be measured. Sharing these expectations with the students constitutes good teaching practice, as they too will know what is expected of them and, more importantly, will develop an awareness of what constitutes a good text.

In the example above only a few teaching points have been focused on, and this risks the impression that the focus is only on linguistic elements. However, the teaching points include other elements such as emotional skills, which in the case of *The Gruffalo* could be related to fear, feeling small or being intelligent. We could also choose to work on reading strategies such as the use of pictures to aid understanding or identify cross-curricular links with arts and crafts, for example. Focusing on these other learning opportunities a text has to offer makes sure that the text is not used as an excuse for presenting a language structure or a set of vocabulary items, as is so often the case in traditional textbook tasks. Rather, while working on a text and developing students' text awareness and linguistic

Table 2.4 Extract from the first page of the planning grid for a unit on *The Gruffalo* including a description of the level of performance expected

	Teaching point	Level expected
Text features (organization of ideas; narrator; use of direct speech; paragraphing; etc.)	Tension through partial description	Students understand the effect of withholding information
Text effect (creating tension; vividness of descriptions; objectivity; coherence; etc.)	Vivid descriptions	
Language functions / structures	Adj. + noun	Students can describe four characteristics of the monster placing the adjective in front of the noun.
Vocabulary	Suggestive adjectives	Students use three less common adjectives.
Pronunciation	Alliteration	Students create one alliteration in their adj. + noun structures
Academic language features		

skills, students develop as learners through a focus on learning and thinking strategies, as well as human beings through the work on culture, their emotional intelligence and their intrapersonal intelligence (values). Finally, identifying links to other subjects in the curriculum allows teachers to create more holistic approaches to learning and avoids the excessive compartmentalization of learning typical of school.

OUTLOOK

In the next chapter we will take a closer look at what a learning path may look like and in doing so examine some important questions about how we work on the reception phase in class.

REFERENCES

Brisk, M. E. (2015). *Engaging students in academic literacies. Genre-based pedagogy for K-5 classrooms.* Routledge.

Derewianka, B., & Jones, P. (2016). *Teaching language in context.* Oxford University Press.

Donaldson, J., & Scheffler, A. (2012). *The Gruffalo.* Macmillan Children's.

Halbach, A. (2018). A literacy approach to language teaching: A proposal for FL teaching in CLIL contexts. *Pulso, 41,* 205–223. https://revistas.cardenalcisneros.es/index.php/PULSO/article/view/310

Martin, J. R., & Rose, D. (2012). Genres and texts: Living in the real world. *Indonesian Journal of Systemic Functional Linguistics, 1*(1), 1–21.

Mickan, P. (2017). Text-based research and teaching. In P. Mickan & E. Lopez (Eds.), *Text-based research and teaching* (pp. 15–35). Palgrave Macmillan.

Wiggins, G., & McTighe, J. (2005). *Understanding by design.* Association for Supervision and Curriculum Development.

CHAPTER 3

Designing the Learning Path: The Reception Phase

Abstract In this chapter, the learning path in the Literacy Approach is looked at in greater detail, focusing on the first phase in a literacy unit: production. At the same time some key issues in teaching foreign languages through text will be dealt with, such as scaffolding students' understanding through the "pre-" stage that leads them into the text and the strategies they need to develop to help them understand texts successfully. At the end of the chapter, the second part of the planning grid is presented as a tool to help teachers plan the learning path.

> *The planning grid helps us to think very carefully about what we want to teach our students and what we want to get from them. (Eva and Marta, primary teachers)*

STARTING WITH THE TEXT

In students' eyes, the work in any literacy unit starts with the text that they view, listen to, watch or read. Not so for the teacher, for whom the phase before the student first meets the text, where the teaching points are identified and the learning path is planned, is the most crucial—and time-consuming—of all. Nevertheless, to understand the logic behind this approach, it is probably easiest if we move through it from the students' perspective, following the learning path outlined in Chap. 2 (Fig. 2.3).

Leading Students into the Text

The first challenge our students will meet in the learning path we have planned for them will be understanding the text, a text which will not be pedagogical in nature like the texts we normally find in textbooks. Rather, in this approach we try to make use of any kind of text that can serve as a model of a given text type, illustrates a number of interesting text features and is appropriate for students' interests and level of maturity. As teachers—and learners—of foreign languages we all know that our skills in understanding are normally much higher than our ability to produce text, an ability that is increased even further through appropriate scaffolding. This scaffolding is often done through *pre-* tasks (pre-reading, pre-listening, pre-viewing), the tasks done before the students actually encounter the text.

However, as Timothy Shanahan (2012) points out, these preparatory tasks have often become discredited as they

1. take up too much time, often being much longer than the comprehension tasks themselves;
2. focus students' attention on the wrong information and
3. give away too much information, making reading, listening or viewing unnecessary.

How can we, then, make sure that the tasks we create to lead students into the text and to aid their understanding are really meaningful?

Again, it is Shanahan who gives us a useful answer: somebody, normally the teacher, has to listen to, watch or read the text in advance, asking themselves what students will find difficult about it and where they may be challenged in their understanding. Once these sources of difficulty have been identified, the teacher can create tasks that address them and, by doing so, will help students deal with these challenges when they meet them in the text. At the same time, these tasks also act naturally as a lead-in to the text and its topic. This sequence of "identifying possible difficulties—doing something about them" lies at the heart of any scaffolding in teaching, i.e. of any temporary help we give students to perform a task they would not be able to do by themselves.

What could the sources of difficulties be for students? Sometimes it may be a cultural element that is crucial to understand a text, e.g., the fact that in certain parts of society in the United States—and to a certain extent in

Europe—being "athletic, tall, and handsome" or "old-money Democrats", like the Sinclairs in the novel *We Were Liars* by E. Lockhart, is a synonym of being successful and popular. In other texts it may be a group of words related to a specific semantic field that may cause difficulties, e.g., some vocabulary related to magic in an excerpt of one of the Harry Potter books. Note, however, that the aim is not for students to be able to understand every single word in the text but rather work on the words that are crucial to understanding the text. This is quite probably more necessary when we work with oral or written texts rather than audio-visual material, where the image goes a long way to aiding students' understanding.

There are endless possibilities for these *pre-* tasks, such as looking at key vocabulary in advance, predicting the content of a story from its title, from the book-cover or from the first frame in a video, but also talking about students' prior experiences in working with a specific text type and what they know about its structure or specific characteristics. The Literacy Approach is rather non-prescriptive when it comes to types of activities, as different tasks may lead to the same result. What is important is that the teacher go through the process of identifying the possible challenges for students' understanding and address them through carefully planned tasks. As in the learning path itself, if I keep an eye on the final aim, i.e. scaffolding students' understanding of the text, I can make sure that every task has a clear purpose and therefore is meaningful and necessary rather than something fun I came up with. Of course, this does not mean that my *pre-* task cannot be fun!

> *I would highlight how flexible the approach is as it allows to implement different activities, making the learning process more meaningful for students. (Isabel, primary teacher)*

Understanding and Enjoying the Text

Once we have led students into the text through the *pre-* task(s), we now turn to working on the text itself, always keeping in mind that the aim is understanding and enjoying. Too often reading, listening or viewing exercises in schools are boring and de-motivating for students, especially in foreign language classes, as they focus students' attention on the "unknown words" they find in the text, e.g., or ask them to remember details from the text after just one look at it.

The first way in which reading, listening or viewing becomes meaningful is by giving students a purpose for engaging with the text: why are they reading, listening or viewing? What is the aim? Finding out more about a historical event or character? Checking whether their predictions were correct? Finding out what happened to Harry Potter in this passage or who the Sinclairs are? Whatever it is we want them to do with a text, students need to know why they are approaching it, and this purpose provides them with a context for their efforts.

In foreign language classes, and in mother tongue teaching to a certain extent, we run the risk of apparently simplifying the understanding process by focusing on the literal meaning of the text. However, to really engage with any text, there are levels of reading that move students' understanding beyond "what the text says" to "what the text means" and "how the text means". These are the three guiding questions of the close reading, or critical reading, approach (Kurland, 1995). Beyond the fact that for readers to develop into critical readers we need to help them move beyond the obvious, literal meaning, working on these other layers of meaning in any text also makes understanding more interesting by giving it greater depth and adding a welcome challenge. This may sound as if it is only relevant to students in secondary school, but in fact primary school children are very well able to understand that the mouse in *The Gruffalo* is making up the monster as a way to protect itself against the bigger animals. We can also expect primary school children to understand that the fact that trees grow in Max's room in *Where the Wild Things Are* (Sendak, 1963) or that dinner is still warm tells us that the story occurs in the protagonist's imagination rather than in reality. It is also not beyond the abilities of younger students to evaluate if an argument is convincing, as anyone knows who has ever been involved in a discussion, even with a young child, about, e.g., pocket money or the need to tidy up.

However, working on the more interesting layers of meaning in a text requires that we help students develop as skilful listeners, viewers and readers, i.e. that we help them develop appropriate comprehension strategies. These strategies include using all the information available in the text for understanding (layout, titles, graphs or illustrations in a written text; pauses, intonation, stress and background noise in an oral text; or images, gestures and music in an audio-visual text; etc.), predict while reading, watching or listening, monitor understanding, visualize what they are listening to or reading or relate the contents and characteristics of the text to other texts they have encountered. This can be done by modelling and discussing these strategies with the students but also through an appropriate design of the tasks students are asked to do while they are watching, reading or listening.

Again, what these tasks look like will very much depend on the text we are working with, as well as on the teacher's preferences, but all the tasks designed need to help students understand the different layers of meaning of the text. This means that often the tasks will focus students' attention on what is relevant, guide their understanding step by step and, through this, help them develop as readers, listeners and viewers.

> *Texts look like a kind of code and we are just giving them the tools to break the code. (Sylvia, primary teacher, Poland)*

Looking at How the Text Means

So far you may feel that the way in which texts are approached in the Literacy Approach is not very different from the way we do comprehension exercises in any foreign language class. And indeed, this may be true of any class where the meaning of the text is at the centre and where understanding is taken beyond the obvious and literal meaning of the text. I, personally, have not seen many classes where meaning is explored in this way, and I have visited a considerable number of classes and worked with many teachers over the years.

Where the Literacy Approach definitely departs from normal classroom practice is in the work done on the question of "how the text means", which we mentioned above as part of critical reading. We do not normally look at the skills of the author in constructing the model text or stop to explore the effect the text has on us and try to identify how this effect is created. This is the focus of the tasks we do in the steps of *observing* and *analysing*. Through these two steps we help students "break the code", as Sylvia, a primary teacher from Poland, aptly put it, and we do so from two different, complementary perspectives: textual and linguistic.

Putting on the Writers' Glasses: *Observing* the Text

In much traditional foreign language teaching, once students have understood (and enjoyed) a text, they are asked to look at the language it showcases—a grammatical structure, a verb tense or maybe a set of new words related to the topic of the unit. This responds to the pedagogical nature of the texts which have often been created to illustrate precisely this language. This is different in the approach we are using here, where texts are chosen because they constitute good models of a given text type, are within the reach of students and will appeal to them. These texts will normally have been created by skilled, professional communicators who can teach us how to use language in communication equally skilfully—at our own level. Therefore, rather than focus on language that has been identified beforehand, language is focused on in so far as it is relevant in the text that is being worked on and is responsible for creating an effect on the reader—thus the importance of starting with the latter, i.e. the effect.

How are the ideas in this text organized? How do you feel when watching this documentary? What is the main idea you take away from this ad? Does this talk reflect the author's opinions or does it present facts? How do you know? These are some of the questions that can guide our work in this phase of the learning path, with some of them focusing on the structural characteristics of the text type that we are using, as captured in Table 2.1 in Chap. 2, and some on the effect of the text on the reader, listener or viewer. In all cases the focus lies on building students' awareness of how the text works, so that it can then be dissected and scrutinized, looking for evidence to back up students' ideas.

This means that students' often unreflected reaction needs to then be pinned down by looking at the text itself, observing it. To move from the students' perception to looking at the actual strategies used by the creator of the text, a student in the master's programme I teach once suggested that students in this phase put on the writer's glasses: they look at the text through the eyes of the skilful, professional creator and try to understand how the effect they have identified is created through the order in which ideas are presented, by providing figures and data, by using a certain image or some strategies to draw the reader into the text. In this MA student's primary class, students actually passed on some glasses when it was their turn to comment on the text.

The work in this *observing* stage takes many different shapes, as it will very much depend on the focus. Thus, e.g., to work on text structure, graphic organizers may be useful, since they act as visual representations of the structure of a text, and each type of text may typically be represented by a different graphic organizer (see Fig. 3.1 for an example). If the focus is on creating suspense, e.g., the exercise will probably be some teacher-guided work on identifying first the effect of the text and then how this is created by the author. Or if what we are looking at is how, in a film excerpt,

Structure d'une explication

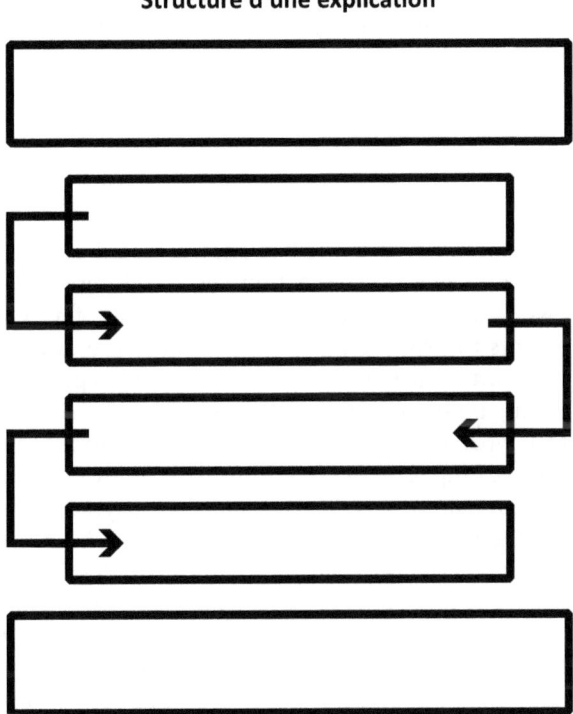

Fig. 3.1 Graphic organizer for explanations, adapted from Brisk (2015, p. 252)

the camera angles help us identify with the main character, we may ask students who they identify with and why. In general, since this kind of work on the text is probably challenging for students, as they will not often have been exposed to tasks that are aimed at building their text awareness, the teacher needs to scaffold this work by focusing students' attention on what is relevant and guiding them to uncover the strategies used by the creator of the text.

When students are looking for evidence in the text, when they have put on the writer's glasses so to speak, at some point they will be zooming in to look at the language used by the creator of the text, so that the work done on the textual features will naturally lead on to the text's linguistic features. This was illustrated in the previous chapter by looking at how the vivid descriptions used in *The Gruffalo* leads the discussion on to looking at alliteration, i.e. sounds and their pronunciation, and vocabulary through the choice of "interesting" adjectives beyond the basic, straightforward "nice", "big" or colour adjectives. This is where we move on to the *analysing* stage and look at the linguistic teaching points as captured on the first page of the planning grid.

Working on the Language: *Analysing* the Text

As we said in Chap. 2, any text type has language features that are particular to it. Thus, in recipes we find action verbs and imperatives, while in descriptions we find verbs of state in the present tense, for example. If we want our students to produce a text of the same type, they will have to become familiar with—at least some of—these language features. These *linguistic* teaching points are easy to identify, as they are shared by all texts of a given text type. However, as we have seen above, language is also responsible for creating an effect, and thus each text we look at will have language features that are specific to it and that may be worth analysing and looking at. Deriving these language features from the effect of the text has the advantage of looking at language in the context of its use—and not any kind of use but skilful, effective use. And this language identified and focused on already constitutes a building block for students' future production and is therefore both relevant and useful for them.

This phase, which in mother tongue teaching could consist in little more than pointing out to students what language the author uses to create a certain effect, will need some more focused work in our model since we are dealing with students for whom the language of the text is not their mother tongue. This constitutes an added challenge for the work proposed here which does not focus on learning the language and even less learning about the language but rather on using it skilfully for real communication. As the challenge is higher, so the support given to students has to be (Mariani, 1997). In practice this means that this is the moment when we will have to look at the order of adjective + noun in the descriptions in *The Gruffalo*, at the pronunciation of the plosives /t/ and /k/ or at the meaning of the adjectives "knobbly", "turned-out" and "poisonous". This focus on vocabulary, in turn, may lead us to discussions about the frequency and specificity of adjectives and to building up word banks with adjectives that are expressive and specific, thus already moving this more language-focused phase towards students' production.

The fact that the language we deal with in this phase comes directly from the text we have selected to work on means that we no longer follow the pre-established order in which vocabulary or grammatical items are supposed to be introduced in the language classes. Rather, students are exposed to language as it occurs naturally and focus on those language items that will be relevant to the texts they have to produce. For some teachers this is an unwelcome departure from the seemingly systematic progression our language syllabi are often characterized by, but research tells us that students do not necessarily learn what they are being taught, nor are they able to use language structures in communication that they may be able to produce correctly in tests (Moeller & Catalano, 2015). This probably coincides with our own experience. We have also probably noticed that even beginning students can learn advanced vocabulary as long as they feel it is relevant for their needs.

Rich input, such as that offered by authentic texts of different types and modes, is likely to help students in their process of figuring out how the language works. However, we also need to make sure that this language is noticed by students and that they then have the possibility to use it in meaningful contexts. On the other hand, research shows us that mastering a language item is not a stage one reaches at any given point but that several versions of the target structure may coexist at any given point in time, leading students to produce correct and incorrect structures in the context of the same text (van Patten, 2020). The text below is a good example of this, with Carlota, a fourth grader, still trying to work out when to use the past tense:

> Scott is going to another country. He was preparing all. His mum was telling him they are late. Five minutes later the bus that goes to the aeroplain was gone and the mum of Scott called a taxi. The taxi was very fast and they were late 2 minutes. Now the new house of Scott was in United Kingdom.

Organizing the Learning Path with the Help of the Planning Grid

It is a long time since we talked about the planning grid in the previous chapter, and you may have forgotten all about it. In Chap. 2 we described how the first part of the planning grid identifies the text type to be worked on in the unit, the source text, the teaching points it offers and the level we expect students to achieve. What we have done up to this point in

Chap. 3 in planning the learning path is reflected in the second part of the planning grid, the one that systematizes the activities in the unit that contribute to getting the students ready to reach the final aim of producing a text of a specific type as skilfully as possible. This second part of the planning grid (see Table 3.1) consists of a series of tables, one for each step in the teaching cycle (see Fig. 2.3 in Chap. 2), grouped into the two phases in which we have divided the work: reception and production. These tables create a space in which the teacher can fill in the information about the tasks that were planned to conform to the learning path: a brief description of the task, the teaching point it addresses, the skills that are being worked on so that we can make sure that students have the chance to practise all four communicative skills, the way students will be grouped to make sure that there is a variety of groupings, the teaching materials that are required and when this task will be done, in which lesson and for how long. Most of these categories will be familiar to any teacher, except for the column of the teaching points.

If you remember, in the first part of the planning grid we identified the teaching points the model text had to offer, and we did so looking at different aspects of the text: textual, linguistic, cultural, strategic, etc (see Table 2.2 in Chap. 2). This is what we want to teach then, and each of the tasks in the learning path will have to address at least one of these teaching points, which are therefore transferred into the second column of the table in the planning grid, identified by the same thick (red) border used in the teaching points table (see Table 3.1). This not only guarantees that the teaching points that we decided to work on are actually dealt with in the learning path but it also assures that each of the tasks planned in the learning path has a clear purpose. As we said when we talked about the *pre-*exercises, our motivation to include any given task in the learning path is not that it is fun to do but rather that it addresses one of the teaching points identified as relevant. Again, this does not mean that it therefore can't be motivating too! In fact, one of the most powerful motivating factors is the perceived relevance itself.

This second part of the planning grid, as was mentioned before, consists of different tables, one for each step in the teaching cycle, and a first one to plan the *pre-* tasks, or, as teachers in the Erasmus+ project said, "to create a hook" so that students are led into the text. However, except for this first introductory phase, this sequence of tables with their corresponding tasks does not mean that the reception phase progresses through

Table 3.1 Second part of the planning grid (blank)

Unit plan

RECEPTION

A. Reading

Phase I. Pre-reading / listening (create hook / open gateway to literacy / contextualize / aid understanding)

Task(s)	Teaching point(s) – refer to table on p. 1	Language skill(s) practiced	Grouping/classroom setup	Teaching materials	Timing / lesson no.

Phase II. Understanding and connecting (literal understanding, inferring meaning, interpreting, relating to own experience, responding)

Task(s)	Teaching point(s) – refer to table on p. 1	Language skill(s) practiced	Grouping/classroom setup	Teaching materials	Timing / lesson no.

B. Observing: recognizing text features (structure, narrator, vivid descriptions, factual information, objectivity of tone…)

Task(s)	Teaching point(s) – refer to table on p. 1	Language skill(s) practiced	Grouping/classroom setup	Teaching materials	Timing / lesson no.

C. Analysing: recognizing and practising language features (language functions, vocabulary, pronunciation)

Task(s)	Teaching point(s) – refer to table on p. 1	Language skill(s) practiced	Grouping/classroom setup	Teaching materials	Timing / lesson no.

(*continued*)

Tabble 3.1 (continued)

PRODUCTION

A. Guided production (ordering parts of text, creating vivid descriptions, making information factual, creating word banks, changing the register, finding and correcting mistakes, etc.)

Task(s)	Teaching point(s) – refer to table on p. 1	Language skill(s) practiced	Grouping/classroom setup	Teaching materials	Timing / lesson no.

B. Free production (planning, organizing, drafting, editing, etc.)

Task(s)	Teaching point(s) – refer to table on p. 1	Language skill(s) practiced	Grouping/classroom setup	Teaching materials	Timing / lesson no.

a series of discrete steps in which the students are first *enjoying* and *understanding* the text, then looking at the effect of the text and finally turning their attention to the language. In practice these steps are neither discrete nor self-contained, so what you do in one stage prepares or asks for something you do in the next. For example, if one of my teaching points is to identify the way ideas are organized in an explanation, while students are watching a video in French about how the voice works ("Comment ça marche la voix?" at https://youtu.be/BxmXBToZHrM), they can already be filling in a graphic organizer with the structure of an explanation (see Fig. 3.1), which they will later use to "observe" the text.

Students can then think about what the producers of the video did to structure the explanations and identify questions as a structuring element, which can further lead them to analysing the form of these questions, only to go back to the video itself and look at how it uses images to underscore the meaning. If we think about it, the three steps in the reception stage should look more like this than like a linear sequence (see Fig. 3.2).

And yet, to make it possible to create a coherent picture of the learning path and make sure that the teaching points we identified are covered, the planning grid describes each of the phases separately. However, the sequence in which these different elements are worked on in the specific learning path can still be captured by situating the task in a specific lesson by completing the last column in the planning grid about the timing and lesson in which the task will be carried out. To continue with the same example about explanations, Table 3.2 shows a short extract of the way the sequence of activities in Fig. 3.2 can be reflected in the planning grid:

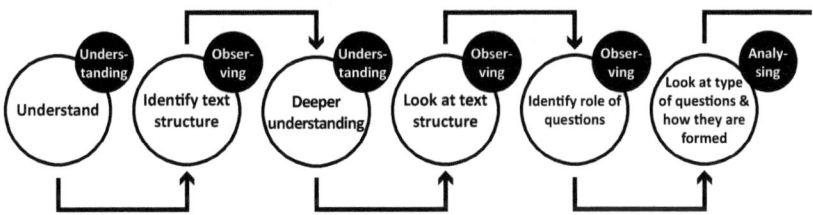

Fig. 3.2 Reception stage in the unit based on "Comment ça marche la voix?"

Table 3.2 Excerpt from planning grid for the reception phase for "Comment ça marche la voix?"

RECEPTION

A. Reading

Phase I. Pre-reading / listening (create hook / open gateway to literacy / contextualize / aid understanding)

Task(s)	Teaching point(s) – refer to table on p. 1	Language skill(s) practiced	Grouping/classroom setup	Teaching materials	Timing / lesson no.
Brainstorming: what do you know about how the ear works?	Predicting	Speaking	Pairs / whole class		Lesson 1, 15 minutes

Phase II. Understanding and connecting (literal understanding, inferring meaning, interpreting, relating to own experience, responding)

Task(s)	Teaching point(s) – refer to table on p. 1	Language skill(s) practiced	Grouping/classroom setup	Teaching materials	Timing / lesson no.
Watch the video to see if your previous knowledge is confirmed; check	Listening for general understanding	Listening	Individual / whole class	Video	Lesson 1, 10 minutes
Fill in the graphic organizer with the structure of explanations	Structure of an explanation	Reading, writing	Individual	Graphic organizer	Lesson 1, 10 minutes

B. Observing: recognizing text features (structure, narrator, vivid descriptions, factual information, objectivity of tone….)

Task(s)	Teaching point(s) – refer to table on p. 1	Language skill(s) practiced	Grouping/classroom setup	Teaching materials	Timing / lesson no.
Collect answers to exercise on graphic organizer and agree on common version	Structure of an explanation	Speaking, reading, listening	Whole class	Graphic organizer	Lesson 2, 10 minutes
Watch the video again to identify how the text moves from one stage to the next	Role of questions in structuring text	Listening, speaking	Individually, whole class	Video	Lesson 2, 10 minutes

C. Analysing: recognizing and practising language features (language functions, vocabulary, pronunciation)

Task(s)	Teaching point(s) – refer to table on p. 1	Language skill(s) practised	Grouping/classroom setup	Teaching materials	Timing / lesson no.
Watch the video and write down the questions you can hear; check with partner	Structure of questions	Listening, writing	Individually, in pairs	Video	Lesson 2, 15 minutes
Analyse the questions and identify their structure (question words, change of word order)	Structure of questions	Speaking	Whole class		Lesson 2, 15 minutes
Create new questions using the same pattern	Structure of questions	Speaking, writing	In pairs		Lesson 2, homework
Correct questions created	Structure of questions	Writing, speaking	Individually		Lesson 3, 10 minutes

Outlook

Having thus worked on planning the reception phase, we are now ready to turn our attention towards students' production, which is the focus of the next chapter. The work students have done on the model text in this phase should enable all of them to produce a successful text in the next phase of the teaching cycle.

REFERENCES

Brisk, M. E. (2015). *Engaging students in academic literacies. Genre-based pedagogy for K-5 classrooms*. Routledge.
Donaldson, J., & Scheffler, A. (2012). *The Gruffalo*. Macmillan Children's.
Kurland, D. (1995). *I know what it says... what does it mean? Critical skills for critical reading*. Wadsworth Publishing.
Lockhart, E. (2014). *We were liars*. Delacorte Press.
Mariani, L. (1997). Teacher support and teacher challenge in supporting learner autonomy. *Perspectives, 23*(2). https://www.learningpaths.org/papers/papersupport.htm
Moeller, A. J., & Catalano, T. (2015). Foreign language teaching and learning. In J. D. Wright (Ed.), *International Encyclopaedia of the social and behavioural sciences* (2nd ed., pp. 327–332). Elsevier.
Sendak, M. (1963). *Where the wild things are*. Bodley Head.
Shanahan, T. (2012, February 21). Pre-reading or not? On the premature demise of background discussions. https://shanahanonliteracy.com/blog/pre-reading-or-not-on-the-premature-demise-of-background-discussions
van Patten, B. (2020). Theories and language teaching. In B. van Patten, G. D. Keating, & S. Wulff (Eds.), *Theories in second language acquisition: An introduction* (3rd ed., pp. 271–290). Routledge.

CHAPTER 4

Designing the Learning Path: The Production Phase

Abstract In this chapter, the focus is on the second phase in a literacy unit: production. We will discuss how to scaffold students' production both through guided work and by working on the process of producing a text. This has implications for the way we assess students' work not only in this production phase but also in the earlier reception phase. Key concepts related to assessment such as formative assessment, assessment as learning or the importance of peer assessment will be dealt with in this context.

> *I used to think that the scaffolding they need to do a writing activity was smaller because I didn't trust that they could do a real writing being 9 years old. [...] I tried that my 9-year-old children did a writing activity about the Moon and the result has been amazing. I created a lot of scaffolding for this and I am so proud of the work they did. It made me realise that scaffolding is not only theory but also real life. (Cristina, primary teacher and MA student, in an assignment)*

Ready for Production

In their progression through the literacy unit, students have had the chance to enjoy and understand a model text, as well as to observe its structure and effect and analyse its language features. This means that, by

© The Author(s), under exclusive license to Springer Nature Switzerland AG 2022
A. Halbach, *The Literacy Approach to Teaching Foreign Languages*, https://doi.org/10.1007/978-3-030-94879-5_4

now, they have identified the features that will make their text successful. That does not, however, mean that they will be able to produce them skilfully or that they will automatically transfer what they have found in the model text to their own production. This is why, as teachers, we need to continue scaffolding students' work. In the Literacy Approach this scaffolding takes different shapes: focusing students' attention on specific features of the text they will have to produce, both textual and linguistic, giving them practice in these features and guiding them through the process of production.

Giving Students the Opportunity to Focus

According to Aída Walqui (2007), one of the main scaffolding strategies consists in focusing students' attention on what is important. Our working memory is limited (Gathercole & Packiam Alloway, 2008), and when we are concentrating on the content of what we want to communicate, we often find it difficult to keep track of our use of the language and even more to use it skilfully to achieve a certain effect. This is why if we want to stretch our students' abilities to produce we need to allow them time to experiment with the language and to focus on specific aspects so that they are then able to transfer what they have learnt and practised in relative isolation to a more extended production.

While you are reading this, you may be thinking that this sounds very much like a PPP (Presentation, Practice and Production) approach (Ur, 1988), where after presenting a given language structure the student practises this structure through grammatical exercises and then—hopefully—transfers it into a free production exercise. While it is true that the sequence *analysis-guided production-free production* resembles a PPP approach, there is a fundamental difference in that the work done in the stages of *observing* and *analysing* is contextualized in the model text that the teacher has selected because it is relevant and interesting to students, and that students have previously worked on to understand it at different levels. Through the work done on the text they have had the chance to develop an awareness of text structure and effect, and students know that what they have learnt will be useful in their own production. They understand what constitutes a good text and what the expectations are for their production.

What *Guided Production* Looks Like

Guided production exercises can take many different shapes, as they focus on various aspects of the text we have identified as teaching points of the unit. Each of these features calls for a different way of working on it, but what exactly the tasks look like, how they are organized and whether they are done individually, in pairs or in groups is up to the teacher to decide. What is important, as usual, is that we keep an eye on the reason why we are doing the task, i.e. on the teaching point it works on, hence, once again, the importance of the initial planning, where the teaching points are identified, and the second column in the second part of the planning grid, which allows us to keep track of how the teaching points are being worked on (see Table 3.1).

To remind teachers how to work on the two phases, *guided production* and *free production*, there are some suggestions in the heading of the corresponding tables (see Table 3.1), but to illustrate how the shape of the tasks will depend on their focus, in the following paragraphs a few ideas are developed further. Thus, if the focus of the task is on the way ideas are typically organized in a text, as, e.g., in the video mentioned in Chap. 3 about how the voice works, students can be asked to organize the paragraphs in an explanation, put different statements forming an explanation into order or sequence the topics dealt with in different sections of a text. If we are adventurous and want to continue working with videos, we could even show them different excerpts of another video of the same series *1 jour, 1 question* (https://www.youtube.com/channel/UCLmlUMA_bGiMWWgfDwfNDgw) and ask them to put them in the right order.

If our model text is *The Gruffalo*, and we want to give students practice in using adjective + noun combinations, a matching exercise could come in handy, or we could do a traditional gap-fill exercise. Once students are familiar with the order in which the adjectives appear, we could increase the challenge of the exercise by asking them to create alliterations, as in the original story: "huge hands", "filthy feet", etc. We could then collect students' examples on the board and decide which of them work and which don't (e.g. brown brain) and why. All these language tasks could be contextualized through some monsters students have previously drawn.

As we said in the previous chapter, since our students are going to produce in a language that is not their mother tongue, we need to make sure that they have access to the language they need and that they do not limit their production to the language that they already know but rather aim at stretching their linguistic resources. There are many resources available, from Internet sites to picture dictionaries, language assistants or the teachers themselves, but in order for the work done locating the linguistic resources to be useful for students during the actual production, it is important to collect this language and make it accessible to them. Word or structure banks, like the one seen in Fig. 4.1, are valuable resources for this purpose.

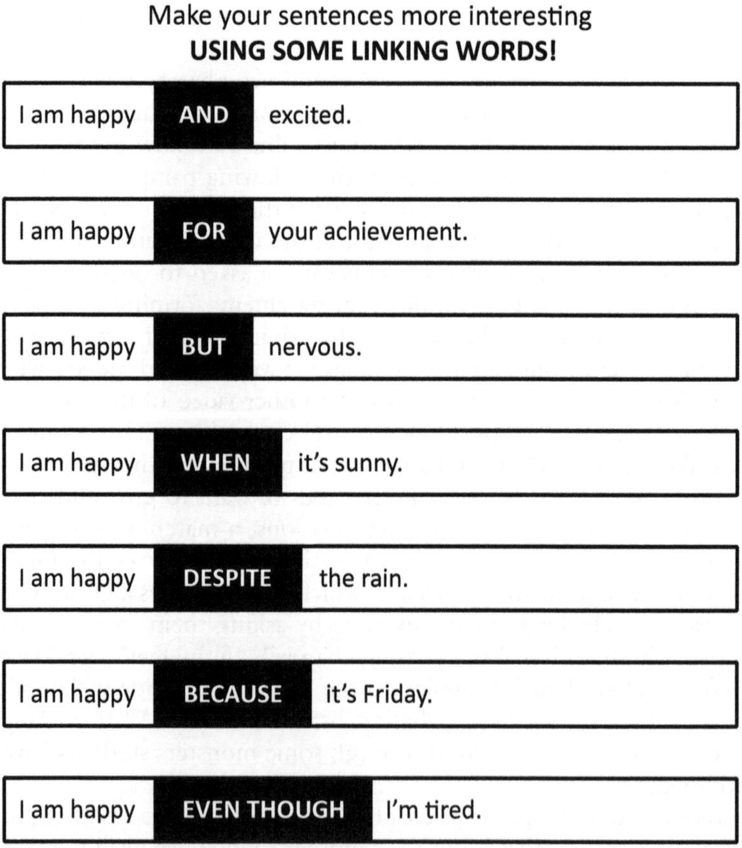

Make your sentences more interesting
USING SOME LINKING WORDS!

I am happy	AND	excited.
I am happy	FOR	your achievement.
I am happy	BUT	nervous.
I am happy	WHEN	it's sunny.
I am happy	DESPITE	the rain.
I am happy	BECAUSE	it's Friday.
I am happy	EVEN THOUGH	I'm tired.

Fig. 4.1 Structure bank

Much of what we have said up to this point about *guided production* exercises may already be well known, but what if our teaching point is related to making a text informative, factual, creating suspense or even using the camera to make the viewer identify with the protagonist? How can we practise any of these? Again, formats may vary, but the key here is to have students experiment, e.g., by trying to make a sentence more informative with the help of questions (see Fig. 4.2).

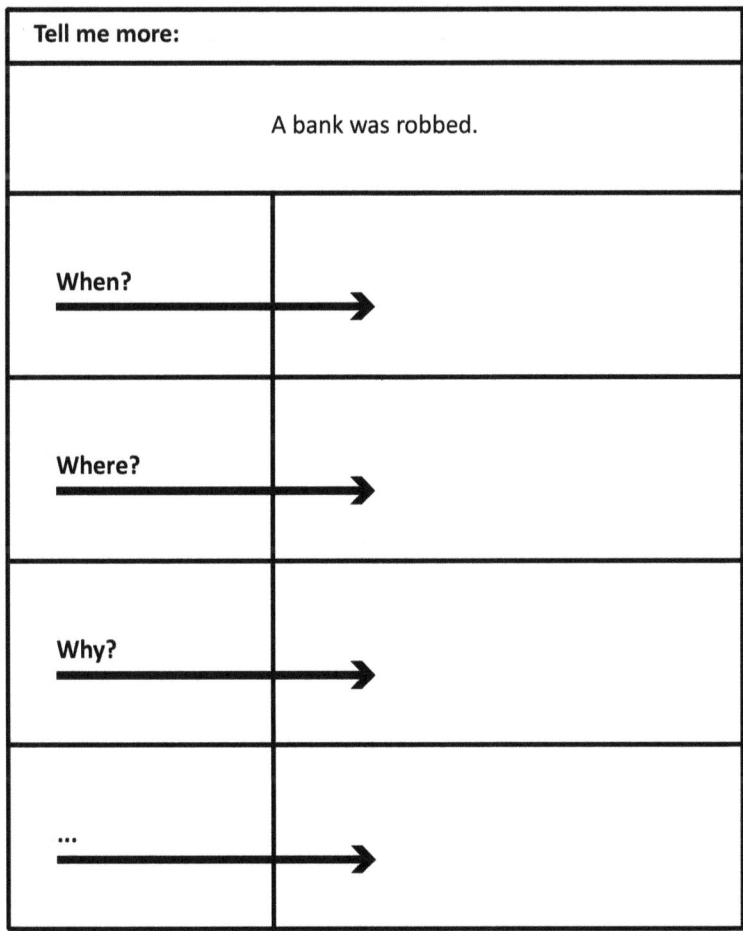

Fig. 4.2 Worksheet: making a text more informative

Practising suspense, on the other hand, will take different shapes depending on the strategies we want to use. For example, we can withhold information, and in this case the type of exercise we can do will be similar to the ones we used to organize the information in the text. We can also use phrases that describe fear or tension through bodily reactions, for which it may be useful to create banks of interesting phrases. These and other strategies may be practised by improving an existing story to make it more suspenseful. And working with a camera to help the viewer identify with one of the characters in a film, e.g., in the scene in Diagon Alley of the first Harry Potter film, can, again, be practised by experimenting. Students can make different takes of the same scene and then evaluate how each one of them makes them feel. They can practise making different takes of the same scene to make the viewer identify with different characters, etc.

What I hope to have been able to explain through these examples is that the focus of this step is not on language per se, and even less on grammatical structures, but rather on whatever textual and linguistic features we have identified in the planning stage as being relevant for successful production. The approach should be playful in the sense of playing around with language—or other elements of text such as illustrations and camera angles—to create an effect and experimenting with different elements to improve the quality of these effects. The awareness of how texts work that students developed in the *observing* stage should now start to be related to students' own ability to communicate skilfully. Again, as was the case with the exercises in the previous steps, the sequencing is not necessarily linear, and the work focused on a certain text feature may come after this feature has been observed (and analysed) in the model text and before the students go back to the model text to look at another one of its characteristics.

TIME FOR *FREE PRODUCTION*

> *Do students in your context find it difficult to "produce" in the English classes?*
>
> *Yes, they do. I would say the reason for it is because it is done mainly at the end of the unit, presented as the "homework" part and students are left alone without support in the process. (Isabel, primary teacher)*

What comes last in the teaching sequence in the Literacy Approach is the *free production*. This should not be surprising, since, as we said in

Chap. 2, the whole learning path that we have constructed through the different tasks aims at making it possible for students to successfully produce a text of a given type. This *free production* exercise, therefore, weaves together all the strings we identified as creating the texture and design of the original text to create a new one. Obviously, we are not aiming at the same level of sophistication as the model texts, but we do want our students to stretch their ability to communicate, and do so not in any way but in the best way possible at their own level.

Guiding Students Through the *Free Production* Stage

However, even though, through the work done up to this point, we have given students the necessary tools for them to be able to produce successfully, this does not mean that we now leave students alone in their production nor that this production needs to be individual and lonely, two of the reasons why production exercises tend to be perceived rather negatively by them. The feeling in this final stage should not be that students are being put to the test but rather that now they have an opportunity to show what they are capable of and to relish in their achievement.

> *I really like the idea of giving my students the time to draft their work. Often, there is not enough time to do this and my students are not always satisfied with their work. My students often feel overwhelmed when it comes to "producing" in English class. Many students will tell me "I can't do it". Giving students the tools that they need to succeed in "producing" is essential for their confidence in learning a new language. (David, secondary teacher)*

The first help we need to give our students is making it possible for them to maintain the focus on the kind of text that they are expected to write. Even in the very simple description of a fantasy dog you can see in Fig. 4.3, the student shows she is aware of the structure of the text, as the text starts with a presentation of the animal (first three lines) and finishes with a comment (last line). This structure is typical of descriptions, and it constituted one of the teaching points the teachers had selected for this unit of work. The next time they work on descriptions, they might want to further develop the students' abilities to write descriptions by presenting a range of sentence structures they can use or teaching them how to group different statements together according to the aspect that is being

Fig. 4.3 Description of a fantasy dog

focused on. A further step in improving students' skills might be to work on expanding each of the sentences to include more information and by doing so make the text less repetitive. This highlights the importance of dealing with any given text type several times, gradually building up students' skills and understanding.

To make sure students don't forget about the nature of the text they are producing, it is good to remind them of all the different text features they have worked on with the help of the model text before they start working on their own production. A written reminder in the form of a wall display may be useful at this stage (see Fig. 4.4), but we could also divide the planning or drafting phase of students' production by following these different steps.

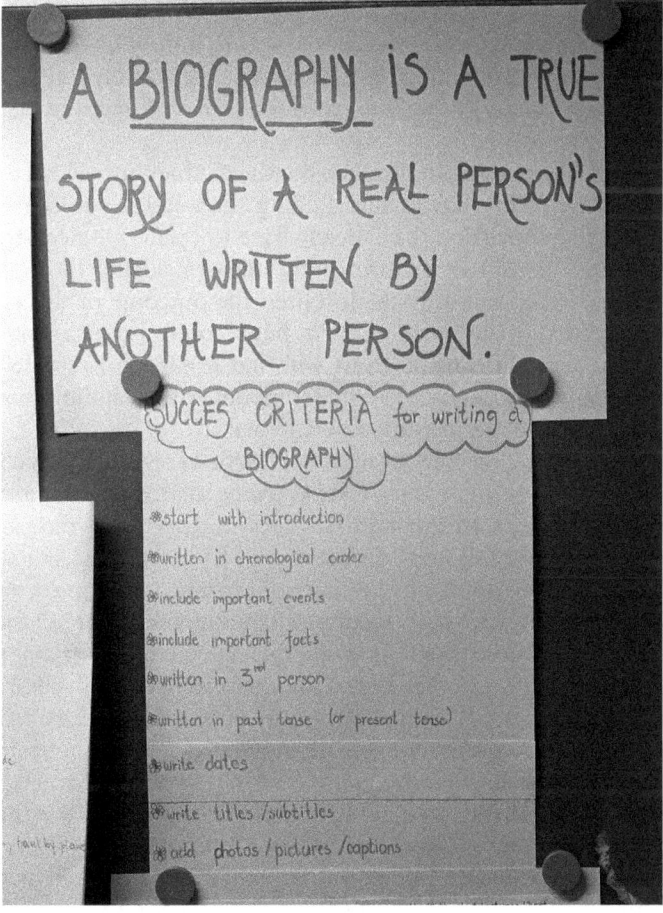

Fig. 4.4 Display reminding students of the purpose and characteristics of a biography

Beyond these reminders, and this help to maintain the focus, in scaffolding students' production we also need to guide them through the process of writing. Even though the process approach to writing has been with us for a long time now (Hedge, 1988), in many classrooms (and textbooks) the production exercises come at the end of a unit of work and are individual tasks that students work on by themselves, often at home. The produced text is then presented to the teacher or class in the case of oral texts, or handed in for correction in the case of written texts. Some students may go to some length to first plan their work and then draft and re-write, but for many others the aim is getting it done as quickly as possible and turning to something else. How can this possibly lead to success if even skilled producers of texts go through different stages to plan, draft and edit their work?

Before actually starting to produce their text, students will have to plan their production. This may involve finding the necessary information or organizing the information they already have to create a logical structure, but it may also consist in brainstorming ideas or talking through one's ideas with a partner to clarify them. Often the outcome of this planning stage is some kind of outline of our text, but it could also be a story board, a flow chart, etc. Different learners will find it easier to represent their ideas in different ways, and different text modes (visual, audio-visual, written or oral) will also require different formats.

Once students are clear about what they want to say and in which order, they will be ready to draft their text, knowing that this first version will never be the final one and that a draft does not start with the first word and end with the last full stop—in the case of a written text. As I am writing this book, I am thinking, writing, re-reading, changing a word or sentence, re-reading a whole section, changing the order of the paragraphs, etc. I also keep questioning whether the ideas I am trying to convey are clear enough, whether I need another example or maybe I should include another figure. With my eyes firmly on my reader, I try to convey information but also make sure you are motivated to keep on reading and find it easy to visualize what this approach looks like. From time to time I stop and ask my husband to be my critical reader and tell me whether what I am saying makes sense. Since this process is repeated several times (much to my husband's dismay!), in Fig. 4.5 this stage is represented as a circle. One of my favourite ways to explain the importance of this process to my students and trainee teachers is by watching a lovely video called Austin's Butterfly (https://www.youtube.com/watch?v=E_6PskE3zfQ), where

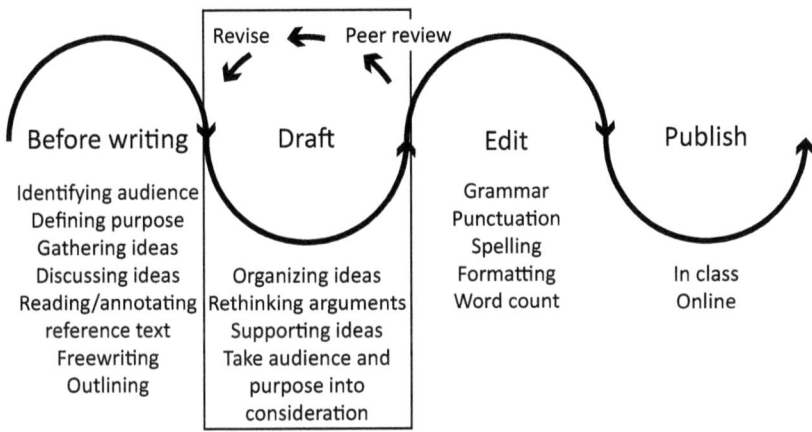

Fig. 4.5 The process of writing

Austin, a first grader, moves from a very basic drawing of a butterfly to producing a really impressive last version through perseverance and by following his peers' very detailed, constructive feedback.

> *What really made me think was the idea of chasing excellence in our students, encouraging them to keep on trying by providing the adequate scaffolding along the process, mainly at production stage. And teaching them not to be content with their first draft but improving their outcome with the help of meaningful feedback and peer collaboration. (C., primary teacher)*

While you are reading this, you may be thinking that this process of drafting only applies to working on written texts, but this is no different when we prepare an oral presentation or a speech, as these modes also require a process of polishing. Here the challenge is to create a good text but then not learn it by heart but rather use it as a springboard for a truly oral presentation—a challenge anybody who ever had to prepare a formal presentation has experienced. Cards with keywords may be of help here.

In this drafting stage the help of a critical reader is very important. However, as teachers we often experience the frustration of seeing students provide very limited, if not straightforward wrong, feedback on each other's work. Often they are shy to critique their peers' work, as they don't want to expose them and have often not understood the importance of giving constructive feedback. Where a positive atmosphere has been created in which students respect each other but are also aware of their role in helping their peers progress, as shown in the "Austin's butterfly" video, they will slowly grow into their role as critical readers.

> *Even the evaluation in this kind of methodology is absolutely amazing, because students evaluate themselves and evaluate each other, so we can work on things like being nice to each other, because the students they can evaluate their friends and they can say nice things about their friends, but they can also be taught to be honest, so we are working in a values kind of way, which I find really important, especially at this age. (Fiona, primary teacher)*

An added difficulty in giving peer-feedback is the fact that often students don't know what makes a text a good text. In the Literacy Approach they can draw on their incipient text awareness to provide meaningful feedback. But even more importantly, through the work done on different text types and their characteristics, students know what constitutes a good production, how the ideas should be organized, what language features should typically appear in the text they have to create, etc. Reminding them of these text features, which were defined as "teaching points" in the teacher's first analysis of the model text, before actually planning the learning path (see Chap. 2), or asking them to focus on some of them in particular, will help students know what to concentrate on when reviewing their peers' work.

The writing process finishes with the editing stage, where such more mechanic aspects as spelling, punctuation and the layout are focused on. This also means that in the drafting stage the attention is on the content, the way ideas are related to each other or an argument is made, and on the effect created in the reader rather than on purely linguistic aspects, which should be corrected in this last, editing, stage. This presents another challenge not only to students in charge of peer-review but also to teachers, as in foreign language classes the attention is often given to precisely these linguistic aspects while the content and the way to create an effect are taken as given or simply ignored.

And once the production is finished? Ideally it will then be shared. Too often the only addressee of our productions is the teacher, who is also the one who looks at the text with critical eyes and duly highlights (in red!) all the mistakes. While feedback and correction are important, so is sharing the work one has taken great trouble to polish and perfect. From a simple display in class to a video channel with the students' book trailers, presenting students' work can take many shapes. This sharing of one's work not only boosts students' self-concept as learners but may also put some slight pressure on them to perform at their best…

Assessing Students' Production

Regarding the school project, although I'd manage to introduce this approach, how effective would it be? I mean, if the evaluation/summative assessment doesn't connect with the methodology, how do I know students are learning? (Natalia, primary teacher)

Like it or not, assessment is an integral part of teaching. Feedback ranks among the elements of teaching with the highest impact on students' performance (Hattie & Clarke, 2018), but assessment should not be equalled with testing. Rather, in line with the idea of the learning path as the gradual development of students' awareness, skills and language that are necessary for successful production, assessment should be formative in nature (Wiliam, 2011), making it possible to identify where students are still struggling and need further practice. On the other hand, the aim of the learning path and the scaffolding we offer students is making excellent production possible rather than highlighting the shortcomings in students' production. And yet, the fact that the first page of the planning grid asked us to define a horizon of expectations for students assures that expectations are consistent and high.

For teachers, focusing on formative assessment means that they have to monitor students' work closely. The discussions of what the text says and means and how it means in the reception phase, as well as the exercises done in the guided production described in this chapter, all provide us with information about students' developing text awareness, skills and language that can be measured against the expectations defined in the planning grid. But even the work done during the process leading towards the actual production (planning, drafting and editing) gives us information about what the students are able—or not yet able—to do. Since students are the protagonists of the learning path, and the work done is largely action-oriented, with students exploring, analysing and experimenting with language, the teacher is free to monitor the work.

The active and progressive nature of students' learning, represented through the learning path, is best captured through the use of a portfolio that includes all the students' work up to the final version of their production: their tasks for understanding the text, *observing* and *analysing* it, their guided production exercises, the various outlines and drafts of the text produced as well as the final production. If this portfolio includes some tools for students' self-reflection, we would also have incorporated *assessment as learning* into our work (Dann, 2002). *Assessment as learning* develops students' understanding and awareness of what they have learnt by asking them to reflect on it with the help of self-assessment questionnaires, to explain what have been the most important things they have learnt in a unit or to select—and justify this selection—a certain number of pieces of work they are especially proud of. This reflection contributes to student growth in "self-regulation, self-efficacy [and] metacognition" (Dann, 2014, p. 150) and is thus likely to help them become more successful learners. This metacognition is also developed through self-assessment questionnaires and checklists (see Fig. 4.6) that help students look at their own production with critical eyes. These checklists can be complemented by the teacher's feedback and should also be part of the students' portfolio.

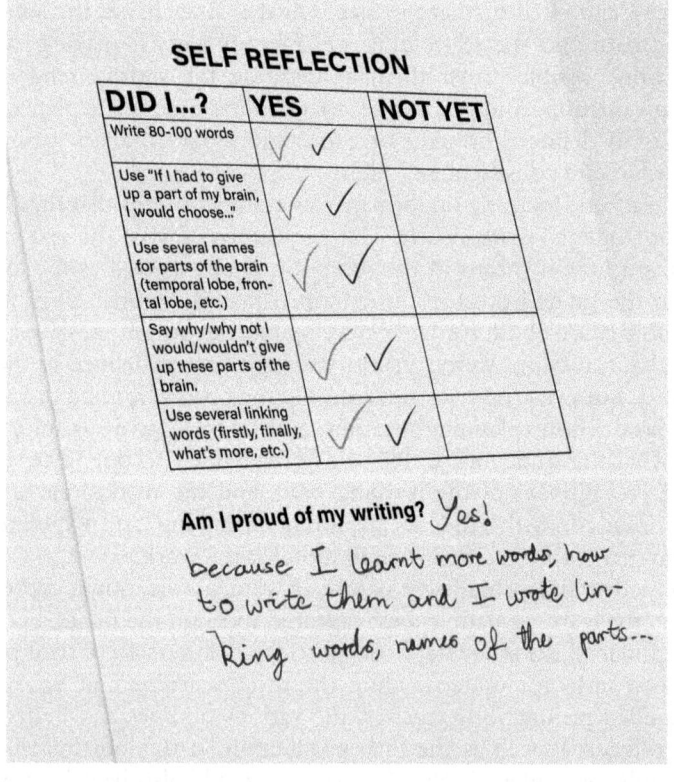

Fig. 4.6 Self-assessment checklist

However, it is not just students assessing their own work but also that of others. The fact that they have had the chance to develop text awareness and are therefore clear about what constitutes a good text makes it possible for students to evaluate their peers' work too. And by doing so, they have a chance to see each other's work, further develop their understanding of what constitutes a good production and "copy" other students' successful moves or phrases.

> *Another idea which I found very interesting is to let students read what others have been writing because it seems an excellent idea to learn from others in both ways: analysing why a particular writing was successful or not, which is also a fantastic way of learning. (Susana, primary teacher)*

Outlook

In the next chapter we will look at a full unit of work for primary students as an example of what working with the Literacy Approach can look like.

References

Dann, R. (2002). *Promoting assessment as learning: Improving the learning process.* Routledge.
Dann, R. (2014). Assessment as learning: Blurring the boundaries of assessment and learning for theory, policy and practice. *Assessment in Education: Principles, Policy & Practice, 21*(2), 149–166.
Gathercole, S., & Packiam Alloway, T. (2008). *Working memory and learning: A practical guide for teachers.* SAGE.
Hattie, J., & Clarke, S. (2018). *Visible learning: Feedback.* Routledge.
Hedge, T. (1988). *Writing.* Oxford University Press.
Ur, P. (1988). *Grammar Practice Activities: A Practical Guide for Teachers.* Cambridge University Press.
Walqui, A. (2007). Scaffolding instruction for English language learners: A conceptual framework. In O. García & C. Baker (Eds.), *Bilingual education. An introductory reader* (pp. 202–218). Multilingual Matters.
Wiliam, D. (2011). *Embedded formative assessment.* Solution Tree.

CHAPTER 5

A Literacy Unit in Primary Education

Abstract In this chapter, a literacy unit for students of Spanish as a foreign language will be presented. As it is based on a video about how to make a paper plane, and there are many of them on the Internet in many different languages, it can easily be adapted to any foreign language class. This unit exemplifies how literacy units work and illustrates how the planning grid can help give shape to this approach to foreign language teaching.

BECOMING CLEAR ABOUT WHAT WE WANT TO TEACH

What does a full literacy unit look like in practice? In this chapter, you will see a literacy unit for students of Spanish as a foreign language focusing on procedure as a text type, and more specifically on instructions. The model text is a video tutorial about how to make a paper plane (e.g. https://www.youtube.com/watch?v=lZYRraIg3no), and this is also the final production we are going to look for from the students. This means that our teaching points are derived from the type of text or genre (instructions) but also from the mode it is presented in (a video tutorial) and the topic it deals with (paper planes). All this information is collected on the first page of the planning grid, as can be seen in Table 5.1.

For example, the fact that this is a set of instructions means that it is structured in different parts, mainly presentation of the product, naming the materials, providing a list of steps and an optional final comment. As

© The Author(s), under exclusive license to Springer Nature Switzerland AG 2022
A. Halbach, *The Literacy Approach to Teaching Foreign Languages*, https://doi.org/10.1007/978-3-030-94879-5_5

Table 5.1 First part of the planning grid for a unit on instructions (Spanish)

Unit overview

Unit:	Text type (narrative, factual description, procedure...):	Text selected
Date:	Procedure – instructions (How to build a paper plane)	Written/oral/visual: audiovisual
Level/age:		Author: "La papelera de Siyon"
		Available at: https://www.youtube.com/watch?v=i2YRraIq3no&t=2s
	= General aim of the unit	

Teaching points – specific aims (as relevant)

		Teaching point	Level expected
Textual	Text features (organization of ideas; narrator; use of direct speech; paragraphing; etc.)	Structure of instructions: greeting, presentation, materials, steps, final comment, goodbye Modelling and explaining Images to help understanding	Students' videos are structured into four parts (greetings & presentation, materials, steps, goodbye) Students accompany the actions in the video with the necessary explanations Students' actions are visible in the video
	Text effect (creating tension; vividness of descriptions; objectivity; coherence; etc.)	Addressing the audience	Students address their audience in the video
Linguistic	Language functions / structures	Giving instructions (imperatives)	Students use half the verbs in the correct form
	Vocabulary	Sequencing: primero, ahora, a continuación, después Semantic field of planes: ala, cola, punta, planear, volar	Students use three different appropriate temporal linkers to sequence the steps. Students use four different words from the semantic field of planes
	Pronunciation		
	Academic language features	Precisión: la esquina superior, el centro, hacia arriba/abajo, por la mitad	Students express the instructions with enough precision to follow them
Cultural			
	Strategic (learning and thinking strategies)	Use images to help understanding	Students are able to follow the instructions in the video
	Cross-curricular links	Arts and crafts (origami) Digital skills	Students are able to use a video camera / mobile phone Students can upload their video on a shared folder
	Emotional skills	De-centring to understand the needs of the audience	Spoken instructions and camera shots take audience into account
	Development of values		

far as the mode is concerned, the fact that on this occasion the text is a video tutorial means that the style is a bit chattier, without losing the necessary precision, and that the viewer is addressed. It also means that the image is crucial to complement the words used and that it is vital for understanding and being able to follow the instructions. Finally, since this video tutorial deals with paper planes, the vocabulary that is used is related to planes (*alas, cola, planear*, etc.) and working with paper (*doblar, marcar, por la mitad*, etc.). Thus the genre, mode and topic all determine the teaching points of this particular unit.

If we now look at the first page of the planning grid (Table 5.1), we will recognize all these elements and a few other aspects that are either necessary for working on this text type or compatible with it, as, e.g., the fact that we will combine this unit with work on origami in the subject of arts and crafts. We will also see that some of the rows in the grid are empty. There may be two reasons for this: either the model text does not offer any teaching point of this particular type (in our case, e.g., working on cultural aspects) or the teacher has decided not to focus on a particular aspect (in this case, pronunciation). However, there are two sections in the planning grid that have to be completed with at least one teaching point: the categories *textual* and *linguistic*. If there are no teaching points in these categories, we will not be working on literacy development.

In the column with the "level expected" you will see that each teaching point is matched with at least one statement of what students can do. The level described here is a minimum pass level and expresses clearly the expectations of the teachers. Sometimes these expectations are very precise and quantifiable; at other times they are less measurable but still need to be expressed clearly and—hopefully—shared with the students so that they too know what constitutes appropriate learning evidence. For the teachers working on this unit, knowing what they are expecting helps to make sure that they have taught everything that students are required to produce—hence the importance of matching each teaching point with the level expected.

From What I Know to What I Could Not Do Alone—The Learning Path

As was mentioned in Chap. 2, the learning path takes students from where they are at the moment when they start working on the unit to the stage where they are able to produce a text—in our case a video tutorial—which they wouldn't have been able to produce by themselves before—at least not with the same level of competence. Along the way, students learn the building blocks of this production as well as its structure, and they develop their skills in using the foreign language to communicate, so that all of them should be able to complete a successful production task at the end of the unit—even though the actual texts produced by the students may look very different, corresponding to their different levels.

As was said in Chap. 3, the first step in a learning path needs to ease students into the model text by activating their background knowledge and working towards making the text accessible through appropriate scaffolding. In this case, the topic is well known, as all students will quite probably have built a paper plane at some point in their lives, but the vocabulary may be challenging, as it is related to specific semantic fields (planes and crafts with paper) and needs to be rather precise to give concrete instructions. Therefore, the first step in the learning path will be to build a paper plane, thereby establishing a link with students' previous knowledge, and talking about it, thus activating the vocabulary students already know and complementing it with new words (see Table 5.2). All these words are then collected in an anchor chart for further reference in the different stages of the unit.

Once students have an entry point to the text, they meet it for the first time. In this case, given the nature of the text, understanding it means that students are able to follow the instructions given in the video. There will be a lot of new words in this text, but since the steps to be taken are modelled by the presenter in the video, the content of the video should be quite accessible. Sometimes students need to be told to focus on the images as, especially in foreign language learning, they tend to be very focused on words. This step in the teaching sequence finishes with students flying their planes in the playground—celebrating their ability to understand a real text in Spanish for native speakers of the language—and comparing how their first and second models fly.

At this point, students have understood the text, but the real work begins now: understanding how the text is structured, how it communicates and what makes it successful. This is what goes on in the *observing* stage and is complemented through the *analysing* stage, which is more focused on the language. Here, students look at the structure of the text (greeting/introduction; materials; steps; final comment/goodbye), at how the image helps understanding, at the phrases used to express sequence and give precision to the description. This may sound very

Table 5.2 Second part of the planning grid for a unit on instructions (Spanish)

Unit plan

RECEPTION

A. Reading

Phase I. Pre-reading / listening (create hook / open gateway to literacy / contextualize / aid understanding)

Task(s)	Teaching point(s) – refer to table on p. 1	Language skill(s) practiced	Grouping/classroom setup	Teaching materials	Timing / lesson no.
Ask students to build a paper plane. Students say a sentence about their plane	Semantic field of planes	Speaking	Individually / whole class	Paper, dictionaries	15' (lesson 1)
Collect words related to planes students have used in the previous task, create anchor chart	Semantic field of planes	Speaking, writing	Whole class	Cardboard for anchor chart	10' (lesson 1)

Phase II. Understanding and connecting (literal understanding, inferring meaning, interpreting, relating to own experience, responding)

Task(s)	Teaching point(s) – refer to table on p. 1	Language skill(s) practiced	Grouping/classroom setup	Teaching materials	Timing / lesson no.
Students follow the instructions on the video to make a new paper plane	Use images to help understanding	Listening, viewing	Individual (if too difficult, stop after each step and give students time to fold the plane)	Video	15' (lesson 1)
Students try out their new paper planes in the playground				Paper planes	5' (lesson 1)
Students compare how their first plane and the second plane fly	Semantic field of planes	Speaking	Whole class	Paper planes	5' (lesson 1)

B. Observing: recognizing text features (structure, narrator, vivid descriptions, factual information, objectivity of tone...)

Task(s)	Teaching point(s) – refer to table on p. 1	Language skill(s) practiced	Grouping/classroom setup	Teaching materials	Timing / lesson no.
Ask students if it was easy/difficult to build the paper plane and why	Structure of instructions Images to help understanding Precision Sequencing	Speaking	Whole class		10' (lesson 2)

(*continued*)

Table 5.2 (continued)

	Teaching point(s) – refer to table on p. 1	Language skill(s) practiced	Grouping/classroom setup	Teaching materials	Timing / lesson no.
Using a graphic organizer, students divide the video into four parts. Discuss the function of each of the parts	Structure of instructions	Listening, viewing, speaking	Individually / whole class	Video	10' (lesson 2)
Ask students if they felt the presenter was nice and friendly and why	Greeting Addressing the audience	Speaking	Whole class		5' (lesson 2)
Ask students to watch the video again and stand up each time there is a new step in the instructions. Ask them how they know	Structure of instructions Sequencing (discourse markers) Images to help understanding	Listening, viewing	Whole class	Video	10' (lesson 2)
Play the sound of the video only and ask students to build a new paper plane. Was it difficult or easy? Discuss what made it so	Precision Images to help understanding	Listening	Individually	Video	10' (lesson 3)
Give students a serviette and give them instructions to fold it into a fan. Don't be precise and don't let them see what you are doing. If they protest, ask them to tell you what you need to improve	Precision Images to help understanding	Listening, speaking	Whole class	Serviette	15' (lesson 3)
As a class, write a list of rules for giving good instructions	Sequencing Precision Images to help understanding	Speaking / writing	Whole class		10' (lesson 3)

C. Analysing: recognizing and practising language features (language functions, vocabulary, pronunciation)

Task(s)	Teaching point(s) – refer to table on p. 1	Language skill(s) practiced	Grouping/classroom setup	Teaching materials	Timing / lesson no.
Collect words and phrases that are used in the video to sequence the instructions. Add them into the graphic organizer	Sequencing	Speaking	Whole class	Video	10' (lesson 2)

Task	Teaching point	Language skill	Grouping	Teaching materials	Timing
Take a sheet of paper and a post-it note with a smiling emoji. Ask students where to place it on the poster, or how to move it	Precision: la esquina superior, el centro, hacia arriba/abajo, por la mitad	Speaking, listening	Whole class	Paper and post-it	10' (lesson 3)
Ask students to find post-its (previously hidden) in the class with expressions from previous task and stick them in the appropriate place of a big sheet of paper	Precision: la esquina superior, el centro, hacia arriba/abajo, por la mitad	Reading	Individually	Big paper and post-its	5' (lesson 3)

PRODUCTION

A. Guided production (ordering parts of text, creating vivid descriptions, making information factual, creating word banks, changing the register, finding and correcting mistakes, etc.)

Task(s)	Teaching point(s) – refer to table on p. 1	Language skill(s) practiced	Grouping/classroom setup	Teaching materials	Timing / lesson no.
Students watch a video of how to make a paper-plane without words	Use images to help understanding		Whole class	Video, e.g., https://www.youtube.com/watch?v=OneYlWOpVcE	5' (lesson 4)
Brainstorm a title for this video		Speaking	Whole class		5' (lesson 4)
Using a graphic organizer to remind them of the structure, students improvise a text for stages 1, 2 and 4	Structure of instructions: greeting, presentation, materials, steps, final comment, goodbye. Addressing the audience	Speaking	In pairs	Graphic organizer	20' (lesson 4)
Using the graphic organizer, teacher creates a shared text for steps 1, 2 and 4 with ideas from students (previous step)	Structure of instructions: greeting, presentation, materials, steps, final comment, goodbye. Addressing the audience	Speaking, writing	Whole class	Graphic organizer	10' (lesson 4)

(continued)

Table 5.2 (continued)

Task(s)	Teaching point(s)	Language skill(s) practiced	Grouping/classroom setup	Teaching materials	Timing / lesson no.
Give students a jumbled text with the instructions in step 3 of the text; students watch the video and re-order	Sequencing Precision	Reading, speaking	In pairs	Video Jumbled text	10' (lesson 5)
Students underline all the important verbs in one colour and the words/phrases used to describe parts of the paper in another colour	Precision Imperatives	Reading	Individually	Jumbled text (now ordered)	5' (lesson 5)
Students make a new paper plane and a partner records them. No words are needed at this stage. Students watch their recordings and evaluate if the angle and distance are good enough for the recording to be clear	Images to help understanding	Speaking	In pairs	Video camera / mobile phone	10' (lesson 5)
Some recordings are shared with the class and characteristics of good recordings are discussed	Images to help understanding	Speaking	Whole class	Students' video recordings	15' (lesson 5)

B. Free production (planning, organizing, drafting, editing...)

Task(s)	Teaching point(s) – refer to table on p. 1	Language skill(s) practiced	Grouping/classroom setup	Teaching materials	Timing / lesson no.
Using a graphic organizer, students draft their script. They refer to word banks and prior exercises as necessary	Structure of instructions: greeting, presentation, materials, steps, final comment, goodbye Addressing the audience Giving instructions (imperatives) Sequencing Precision	Writing	Individually	Graphic organizer	20' (lesson 6, or homework)

Students give instructions to a partner who follows them to make sure the instructions are clear. Each time the partner is unclear, the student marks it in his/her draft	As above	Speaking, listening	In pairs	Paper for planes	15' (lesson 6)
In pairs students work on the marks in the drafts to improve precision	As above	Reading, speaking, listening, writing	In pairs		10' (lesson 6)
Students rehearse the instructions and the modelling several times with different partners and receive feedback	As above Images to help understanding	Speaking, listening	In pairs		15' (lesson 6)
In pairs, students record their videos as often as necessary until they are satisfied with the result	Images to help understanding Digital skills	Speaking, listening	In pairs	Video camera / mobile phones	20' (lesson 7)
Videos are shared with another class who join the students in the playground for a contest of paper planes	Digital skills				10' (lesson 7)

academic for a unit that we will quite probably work on with primary students, but these students also like to be challenged from a cognitive point of view, and a stage like this can still include work through movement and action. The key is that students are engaged and that there is some variety in skills involved and grouping, so that phases where students work by themselves or in pairs are combined with others in which the work is more teacher-led.

Another characteristic of the Literacy Approach that is important is that the teaching starts from students' experience of the text and that it helps them reflect on the nature and the effect of this text. Students don't need to be told *about* the text but rather need to discover how it works by themselves, taking an active role in the process. This is why the learning path includes an exercise where students are challenged to follow instructions to fold a serviette without visual support, so that they experience how important the image is (see Table 5.2). Once students are clear about, in this case, the importance of the image, they are ready to create meaningful rules for good instructions on video.

Finally, as can be seen in Table 5.2, each of the more textual features of the model used is analysed in terms of the language features—or the features of the video—that are accountable for it. So, e.g., when thinking about the precision of the instructions, students will discover that it is the result of using expressions that indicate what parts of the sheet need to be folded and where (*la esquina superior, el centro, hacia arriba/abajo, por la mitad*). Once they have become aware of the importance of these expressions, students look at their meaning. This means that each of the teaching points identified in the *textual* section of the first page in the planning grid needs to be analysed from a linguistic point of view. This is especially important because our learners are not native speakers of the language, and they therefore need extra work on the language, in terms of both vocabulary and language structures. The same would be true for students form whom English is an additional language (EAL) learners (Lin, 2016). We need to make sure they develop their language skills and repertoires so that they can then produce their own texts skilfully. Since the planning grid distinguishes between *observing* and *analysing* to make sure both are covered and attention does not directly turn to the language, as is often the case in "traditional" EFL classes, it becomes a bit difficult to make the correspondence between the textual and the linguistic clear, so readers are referred to the last column in Table 5.2 to look at the lessons each of the tasks corresponds to. You will notice that the first task in the analysing stage is actually placed in lesson 2, while from the fifth task in the *observing* stage onwards we are located in lesson 3.

Once students have understood the text and looked at how it works, they are ready to start producing, but, as was said in Chap. 2, this production still needs to be guided. In this section of the planning grid (Table 5.2) you can see how students are taken step by step through different tasks that focus on different aspects of their production. They create a new text together, focus their attention on the sequencing of the different steps in the instructions and highlight important words they might want to use in their own production. They also experiment with the camera, trying to find the best angle to record their own instructions. Since mobile phones and video cameras are very much part of our students' lives, many of them will not need to learn how to use them or how to upload their files once they have produced their final versions, but we need to be ready to support the less techy students.

Once students have had the possibility to prepare for their own production in this way, they are ready to start working on it. It is important to note, once again, that this is not linear work where students grab a camera and start recording but rather a longer process where students start with a draft, try it out on their partners, note where the text does not work, improve the draft with the help of the partner, rehearse their instructions with several partners, and only then start recording. But even this recording is not final, as students are allowed to repeat it as many times as necessary: the aim is for everybody to create a product that they can be proud of, and not to catch students out on what they are not able to do, as is so often the case. And because students can work on their product until they are satisfied with it, they will be able to share a piece of work they can be proud of. The fact that these recordings are shared with another class may also motivate those students who would rather hand in the first version and be done with it to be a bit more patient and strive for excellence. Finally, since the other class these videos are shared with will build the paper planes following the instructions, feedback on the way the videos communicate is automatic and guaranteed.

I have recently been following an exchange on Twitter where a teacher was reflecting on motivation and how what really motivates students is the feeling of knowing what they have to do and how. This is what Deci and Ryan (1985) call "competence", and it is one of the requisites for motivation to develop. According to them we all have the innate drive to grow but need the context to foster and encourage this growth. By giving students the necessary understandings of text and tools for creating their own texts successfully, we are developing their competence and thus contributing to making this growth possible. How often have we used external rewards to motivate students only to find that they are short-lived? What really motivates is this sense of expertise—together with the other two factors Deci and Ryan identified: autonomy (or the feeling of having control over what we do) and relatedness (or the feeling of belonging to a group of persons).

OUTLOOK

Now that we have had the chance of looking at a complete unit of work, which has hopefully helped to bring the Literacy Approach alive, we can turn to one of the main concerns of most teachers: how to make this approach compatible with the existing language curriculum.

REFERENCES

Deci, E. L., & Ryan, R. M. (1985). *Intrinsic motivation and self-determination in human behaviour*. Plenum.

Lin, A. (2016). *Language across the curriculum & CLIL in English as an additional language*. Springer.

CHAPTER 6

Integrating a Literacy Approach Into an Existing Curriculum

Abstract This chapter focuses on long-term planning and on how to align literacy units with the existing curricula for EFL. It then suggests a way in which the work through the approach can be integrated in an existing syllabus and describes two curricula that were designed specifically to develop literacy in the foreign language classes.

BUT I HAVE A CURRICULUM TO FOLLOW …

At least in my context, one of the great worries of teachers is related to the fact that they have a foreign language curriculum to cover. There are certain grammatical structures that students need to know (and be able to use?) and certain vocabulary items that they need to be familiar with. They have to practise certain skills and be able to talk or write certain kinds of text, mainly narrative. This pressure is even stronger when students are regularly examined through high-stakes external examinations, and schools are then evaluated in terms of the results achieved by their students. For many teachers this means that they are not only bound by the curriculum but they actually feel they have to teach to the test, making sure students are ready for it. In this context, departing from the way the foreign language is normally taught is difficult.

© The Author(s), under exclusive license to Springer Nature Switzerland AG 2022
A. Halbach, *The Literacy Approach to Teaching Foreign Languages*, https://doi.org/10.1007/978-3-030-94879-5_6

This becomes even more complicated because we are used to taking the contents and skills the curriculum identifies as a starting point for our planning. However, if you remember in Chap. 2 we described the approach to planning units of work in the Literacy Approach as starting from the back or using backward design. The first step in the planning of a literacy unit is the final production task: a given text type in a given mode and with certain structural and stylistic characteristics. So the starting point is not the contents and skills but rather what I expect my students to be able to produce at the end. Having said this, as in any other teaching unit, in the literacy units students have an opportunity to develop their skills and learn different contents, as I hope to have shown in the previous chapters. This means that the items we normally find in a syllabus are there, but not as a starting point in the planning—at least normally—but rather as elements that naturally emerge from the work done on texts. What needs to be done then is match these naturally emerging opportunities for language-focused work and for skills development against the existing curriculum.

If you think about it, in the first part of the planning grid we already identified the contents that are going to be covered in terms of the language focus, the learning strategies, cultural elements, etc. In the second part of the planning grid, the skills worked on are identified in the column labelled "Language skill(s) practised" (see Table 3.1), so this document already identifies the skills that are being covered in the unit. If we now turn all the elements of the curriculum into a checklist (see Table 6.1), we can tick off those that are covered by the unit we have designed. This allows us to identify what contents have been dealt with but also which ones still need to be worked on and plan accordingly.

Experience shows that teachers are normally surprised by the number of items from the curriculum they can tick off after any single unit of work with the Literacy Approach. In fact, the ticks you can see in Table 6.1 correspond to the communicative skills as well as the grammar and the vocabulary covered in the reception stage of a unit developed for year 10 students on *We Were Liars* (see Appendix A for a unit plan and Appendix B for a complete checklist of contents to be covered in year 10 in bilingual schools in the Comunidad de Madrid). However, the learning in this unit is not limited to these items from the curriculum but also includes cultural elements such as the prototype of a successful American family, an

Table 6.1 Items from the curriculum for Advanced English (year 10) for bilingual schools in the Comunidad de Madrid, Spain (Madrid, 2018), covered in the reception phase of the unit on *We Were Liars*

	Covered in the unit
Listening	
Classroom interaction with teachers and peers	√
Speaking	
Participation in daily interaction in the classroom, especially in pair and group work as well as in interaction with the teacher	√
Participation in discussions: presenting one's own opinions accurately, refuting the opinions of others, asking for clarification, asking questions, etc.	√
Ability to deviate from the prepared script in discussions and presentations to respond to interventions of other participants or requests for clarification	√
Ability to initiate, maintain and complete conversations in more or less formal contexts and to repair problems that may arise through repetition, paraphrasing or clarification	√
Ability to respond to questions and requests for clarification or repetition and correct errors if they have led to confusion	√
Effective use of connectors typical of spoken language to identify the relationship between ideas	√
Ability to summarize what has been heard by way of clarification	√
Ability to use synonyms, approximations and paraphrases in situations where he or she does not know a particular term.	√
Pronunciation, accentuation, intonation and rhythm without errors that could lead to confusion	√
Reading	
Anticipation of content in literary, argumentative and opinion texts with different levels of formality	√
Ability to adapt reading strategy to the characteristics of the text and the needs of the task (skimming, scanning, extensive reading, intensive reading)	√
General and detailed comprehension of literary, argumentative and opinion texts with varying levels of formality	√
Understanding the effect and meaning of stylistic elements and discursive strategies in literary and non-literary texts (irony, metaphor, personification, generalization, etc.)	√
Ability to identify and analyse the role of fictional elements (location, characters and narrative) in literary texts of different genres (narrative, poetry and drama)	√
Inference of points of view and opinions which are not expressed openly	√
Supporting interpretations of the meaning, effect or quality of a text with evidence taken from the text	√

(*continued*)

Table 6.1 (continued)

	Covered in the unit
Language functions: use of the following linguistic functions at an intermediate-advanced level, both orally and in writing	
Describe: *There is/there are …; The first impression we get of X is …; Its main characteristic is …*	√
Construct understanding building on other people's: *My idea/explanation is similar to/related to …; My idea builds upon X's idea that …; I agree but would phrase it a bit differently/add something else/look at it from a different perspective*	√
Justify: *The reason is …; This can be seen from …; I believe this because …; My primary reason for thinking so is …; Perhaps the most convincing reason for thinking so is …*	√
Give opinions, rebut: *Based on my experience, I think/believe that …; In my opinion …; As for me …; I don't agree …; I see your point, but …; Unlike X, I think/believe that …; I see it differently…*	√
Asking for opinions: *What do you think? Do you agree? What about you? What do you make of this? What is your take on X?*	√
Asking for information/clarification: *Something else I'd like to know …; Could you be more specific about this? If I have understood correctly, your point is that …; Sorry, but I'm not (quite) clear on …; In other words, you think …*	√
Paraphrase: *So you are saying that …; What I hear you saying is that …; In other words, you think …*	√
Analyse: *We can interpret X as …; Given the evidence, we can deduce that …; X is related to Y in so far as …; We can draw parallels between texts/characters/the setting and the narrative because …*	√
Present interpretations tentatively: *X seems to indicate that …; X could be interpreted as meaning …; We could assume X to mean …; This would mean that …*	√
Present arguments: *Based on the evidence presented so far, I believe that …; The advantages of … outweigh the disadvantages of … insofar as …; Although some people claim that …, opponents argue that ….*	√
Finish argumentations: *At the end of the day …; Summing up …; Having reached this point …*	√
Grammatical structures	
Complex conditional structures: *should, only if,* and *as if/as though*	√
Lexis	
Use of common expressions, lexis and fixed phrases about topics of general and personal interest, everyday topics or contents of other subjects in the curriculum	√
Recognizing synonyms, antonyms and *"false friends"*	√

(*continued*)

Table 6.1 (continued)

	Covered in the unit
Use of a variety of linkers: *due to; so; though; unless; so as; in order not to; however; on condition that* ...	√
Understanding common academic vocabulary according to the *Academic Word List*, such as: *achieve; affect; appropriate; aspects; categories; chapter; complex; conclusion; consequences; cultural; design; elements; evaluation; features; final; focus; impact; items; obtained; perceived; positive; potential; previous; primary; region; relevant; resources; restricted; sought; select; strategies; survey; text; traditional; transfer*	√
Pronunciation	
Using appropriate rhythm, intonation, sentence and word stress	√

awareness of irony as a stylistic resource and, very importantly, the development of language awareness.

Experience also shows that in countries like Spain, where textbooks often take the role of the curriculum, teachers find it difficult to free themselves from the temporal sequence in which the contents are presented in the textbooks. I have seen teachers including items in the teaching points table not because the text offered them but rather because the textbook unit they would be teaching normally included this particular content. This happens particularly often with language items and compromises the focus on literacy development, as these language items are no longer part of a text or contribute to the way it makes meaning. To avoid this, it will be best to look at all the texts we want to work on during a given year together and identify what they offer in terms of teaching points. Should we still find that some elements from the curriculum are missing, we can always look for a text that offers, or is at least compatible with, the missing elements. This still means that we are working with text types as the organizing principle of our planning, since what the model text is about specifically, how it communicates or what skills it requires are rather open and can be adapted to the requirements of the curriculum.

A Whole School Approach to Literacy Development

In English we are doing argumentative texts now. It's frustrating because we already did them last year in Spanish! (Juan, tenth grade student)

As was mentioned in Chap. 4, text types are not learned in one go but need to be revisited several times for students to develop a good understanding of how they work as well as increasingly sophisticated ways of expressing meanings. As we saw in the example of the description of a fantasy dog (Fig. 4.3), the student had understood the structure of the description, but the text was still a collection of independent statements about the dog that all followed a similar structure. On next dealing with descriptions, the students would need to learn how to construct a coherent text, order the different elements in the description in a meaningful way and use a variety of sentence structures. However, gradually building up an understanding of text types and the corresponding skilful use of language requires a high degree of coordination and shared planning, especially since it is likely that different teachers will work on the same text type with the same group of students at different moments in time.

But not only that, most of our students are likely to be learning more than one language in school, and while each language communicates in slightly different ways, as does each subject discipline (chemistry, history, etc.), there also are a lot of shared aspects that do not need to be re-taught in each of the languages. Juan, the secondary student in the quote above, had recognized this and expressed his frustration at the fact that teachers were not taking this prior learning into account but rather were starting from scratch. This means that the coordination mentioned above needs to cover the different languages in the curriculum as well as the different types of text.

A school I work with was aware of the need to change the way they were dealing with the languages in their teaching and created a committee of teachers to develop a curriculum to cover the six years of primary education and the three languages in the curriculum: Spanish, the main language of the context and for most students their mother tongue; English, the first foreign language that was taught from infant education onwards (students aged three) and used for part of the content subject teaching in primary education; and French, starting in the fourth year of primary.

Using text genres as the main organizing principle of their curriculum, they created a genre map spanning the six years of primary education. In Table 6.2 you can see what their distribution of genres looked like. This is very obviously not the only way to work with this idea—if only because the conceptualization of the genres is rather wilful (letters and emails can narrate, describe, argue or persuade, e.g.). But it does show a clear progression in the work done, with the easier or more familiar genres coming in the first years and the more complex ones being dealt with in the higher grades. It is also interesting to see how writing in French, the second foreign language, is introduced starting with very formulaic text types (e.g. poems) or those that require less language, like comics, and that any given text type is dealt with several times during the schooling. You will also see that often the same genre is worked on in all languages of the curriculum. This will allow for easy transfer of learning from one language to the other but is, of course, just one possible option. We could also think of going back to the same genre in different languages at different times.[1]

In this same school the fifth grade teachers decided to work in a topic-based way, so that all three languages would work on a shared topic as well as on the same genre. This means that the same semantic field, as well as the same genres, are dealt with in the three languages, resulting in students' production like the ones seen in Figs. 6.1, 6.2 and 6.3. The level of scaffolding provided by the teacher as well as the level of complexity of the text produced will vary according to students' proficiency in the languages, but all three texts deal with the topic of magic, and those in Spanish and English, the two stronger languages, are clearly poems.

Working in this coordinated way allows students to transfer what they learn from one language to another but also to perceive the curriculum as a whole. This makes for more meaningful learning and allows students to develop strategies for transfer and resourcing that will be helpful for their learning in all subjects.

---

[1] Similarly, but much wider in scope, the Australian curriculum identifies the genres in the different content subjects and, again, distributes them throughout the ten years of obligatory schooling. The resulting genre maps are available at https://sapsp7.weebly.com/uploads/2/4/7/3/24735495/genre_maps_of_the_australi.pdf

Table 6.2 Distribution of genres across the six years of primary education including the three languages in the curriculum

		1st			2nd			3rd			4th			5th			6th		
		Sp	Engl	F	Sp	Engl	F	Sp	Engl	F	Sp	Engl	F	Sp	Engl	F	Sp	Engl	F
Writing single words and simple sentences		■																	
Poems											■	■							
Narrative	Structure (introduction of character and setting, complication, resolution)										■	■	■						
	Setting (time and place)																		
	Description (persons, animals, places and objects)	Oral and read																	
	Story / Legend / Myth	Story						Fable						Legend			Myth		
	Biography																		
	Diary																		
	Anecdote	■	■			■													
Letter (Invitations, messages, e-mails, etc.)																	Email	■	
Summary									■								■	■	
Outline (Main ideas, secondary ideas, etc.)								Guided									■	■	
Comics															■		■	■	
Interview																	■	■	
Dialogue					Recipes												■	■	
Instructions						■			■										
Argumentation																			
Report																			
Newspaper article																			
Chronicle																			

Fig. 6.1 Poem about witches in Spanish

Fig. 6.2 Poem about vampires in English

Developing an English Curriculum That Feeds into the Content Subjects

Using a literacy-based approach like the one described in this book is especially important in contexts where the foreign or second language is the language in which all or some of the content subjects are taught, i.e. in Content and Language Integrated Learning (CLIL) programmes or programmes for students whose mother tongue is not the language of schooling, e.g., EAL students. In these contexts, students will depend on

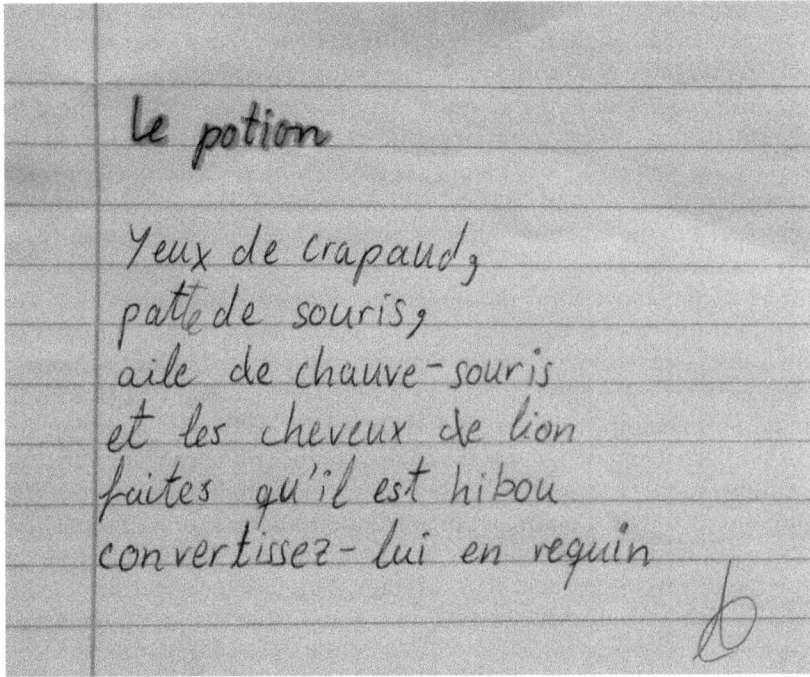

Fig. 6.3 Rhyming recipe for a magic potion in French

understanding and producing text in the foreign or second language for their content subject learning. Familiarity with different text types will therefore be crucial for them to succeed academically. Unfortunately, content subject teachers are often not able to help students develop this vital understanding of texts and ability to communicate skilfully—partly because their curriculum is already crammed but often also because they themselves have not had the opportunity to develop the necessary text and language awareness. This is where integrating the language subjects with those that focus on contents becomes very important.

If we analyse the content subject curricula, it should not be too difficult to identify the text types they require students to produce. These text types can then be dealt with in the language subjects, with the content subject teachers just focusing on what is particular to the language of their specific subjects. This, however, does not mean that language teachers start working on contents which they may not be familiar with, as in Content Based Language Teaching (CBLT; Cenoz, 2015), but rather that the text types are dealt with in their non-subject specific variety. For example, instructions for doing an experiment in science can be transferred to the language classroom as a recipe. The structure and language will not be exactly the same, but what students learn from working on the recipe about the structure and characteristic elements of this text type can be transferred to the experiment instructions, with the necessary guidance on the teachers' part.

All of the above form the underlying idea of a curriculum that was designed for—and is currently being implemented in—the four years of obligatory secondary education and the two years of higher secondary education for the subject of "Advanced English" taught in CLIL schools in the autonomous region of Madrid (Halbach, 2020). The starting point for the curriculum design was the analysis of the content subject curricula of those subjects taught in English—most notably history and geography—to identify the text types they required students to produce. These text types were then grouped by year and "translated" into non-content specific text types. For year 8, this meant, e.g., that the scientific description students would have to understand and write in their physics and chemistry classes was turned into a description of an object or the description of a literary or fictional character (see Table 6.3). The structure students would learn for their descriptions of objects and characters would also be valid for the description of scientific equipment or the structure of an atom, for example.

Once these text types had been identified and "translated" into ELT, they were matched with the academic skills that the work done on this particular text type would require or be compatible with. In a final step, the descriptors of the communicative skills according to the CEFR level required for year 8, in this case B1+, that matched the text type were selected and assigned to the different text types. This does not mean that the same skills—academic or communicative—were not worked on elsewhere in the curriculum, as skills are developed over time and through frequent practice.

This curriculum provides teachers with a general guideline for work, but it is still necessary for them to work from the text chosen as a model, identify the teaching points and develop the learning path from there, as described in Chap. 2 of this book. The sources provided in the last column help teachers find an appropriate model text coming from a film (*Harry*

Table 6.3 Extract from the syllabus for Advanced English, year 8, description

Text type and structure	Examples of texts	Reading	Writing	Listening	Speaking—interacting	Thinking	Possible source of text
Description: (1) Classification (general statement) (2) Description (3) Concluding comments (evaluation)	• Character description (fictional and literary) • Description of objects, possessions and products (letter of complaint/phone conversation about a malfunctioning product)	• Understand simple literary and non-literary descriptions (of characters/objects) • Identify and understand basic stylistic devices and their effect/function: metaphor, comparison, exaggeration, irony • Critically evaluate the effectiveness of a description • Identify the descriptive strategies used to describe a character	• Describe a fictional or real character • Write a literary characterization • Use evidence from a text to support a literary description • Express a complaint about a malfunctioning product, describing it in detail • Write comments and complaints about products and services	• Understand a consumer-related problem when described by somebody • Identify the descriptive strategies used to describe a character • Understand the meaning and effect of stylistic devices in description: irony, metaphor, simile	• Describe objects, possessions and products in detail, including their characteristics and special features • Describe an everyday consumer-related problem and request a correction or solution • Describe a real or imaginary person with some degree of detail	• Use model texts to help write a new one • Use evidence from a text to back up a literary description • Quote appropriate passages of text and insert the quotes into the description • Understand the difference between a literary and a fictional description	• 39 Clues by Rick Riordan • Harry Potter by J. K. Rowling • Sherlock Holmes by Sir A. Conan Doyle (also as BBC series) • Holes by Louis Sachar Poems: • The Eagle (Alfred, Lord Tennyson) • Ozymandias (Percy Bysshe Shelley) • Sorting Hat poem from Harry Potter and the Sorcerer's Stone

Potter and the Philosopher's Stone), a TV series (*Sherlock Holmes*), a novel (*39 Clues*) or a poem, such as "The Eagle" by Alfred, Lord Tennyson. Again, these sources are suggestions rather than a mandatory text.

The actual text teachers choose to work on will determine the teaching points they will deal with in the unit, with respect to not only the skills work and the language work but also the textual features and the learning skills. While this "indetermination" quite obviously requires much more work from the teachers than following a textbook, as they need to plan their unit of work, experience shows that it also contributes to making the teaching better, as teachers have thought through the unit in a completely different way from what they would do when using pre-constructed units of work. The planning grid that captures their planning for the unit is perceived as a tool that is really useful for teaching.

> *My syllabus design for English usually ends up in the drawer or on the shelf, but the planning grid was always in my hands. (Ana Esther, primary teacher)*

At the same time, the challenge implied in developing one's own units of work is actually motivating for teachers. On the one hand, they feel empowered, because they no longer depend on the textbook for their teaching; they can put their creativity into their unit plan and—to a certain extent—can choose texts that they themselves find appealing. At the same time, the experience of being able to face the challenge is motivating in itself, and seeing the effect the units have on students' motivation and learning in turn strengthens teachers' motivation. From a practical point of view, once units have been developed, they can be used with different groups of students, adapting them to their specific needs, as would be done with traditional textbook units. Finally, teachers can cooperate by sharing the units they have planned, or by working on the planning as a team, which will probably distribute the work effort and result in a better school climate and higher motivation on the teachers' side.

LANGUAGE TEACHING AS PART OF STUDENTS' ACADEMIC DEVELOPMENT

The examples of foreign language curricula provided in this chapter—one distributing the text genres across the primary education stage and the other working on the texts required by the content subjects taught in English—illustrate how, by organizing the teaching around text types, foreign language teaching is no longer separate from the other subjects in the curriculum but rather contributes to achieving the learning goals across it. In the curriculum for primary education, literacy is developed across languages, which not only allows teachers to draw on each other's work and therefore save time but also helps students develop their metalinguistic awareness as they transfer what they learn in one language to the other or compare how different languages work. This same awareness will contribute to developing their understanding of text and therefore make students more skilful in understanding and producing texts. Finally, the joint work in the different languages of the curriculum contributes to creating a more holistic perception of learning for students and fosters the transfer of what is learnt in one subject to the other.

This same transfer of learning will occur in the curriculum for Advanced English, as students make use of what they learn in the subject of English in their content subjects taught in English. However, this process does not necessarily occur spontaneously (Bransford et al., 1999), so teachers will have to draw students' attention to the need to do so. This ability to make use of knowledge and understandings from different disciplines is one of the characteristics of the deep learning our knowledge society requires (Pellegrino & Hilton, 2012).

But working in this way also requires content and language teachers to cooperate, as they have to identify the text types required in their subjects. This offers content subject teachers a chance to develop their own language awareness. It also highlights the importance of language and meaning-making in learning any subject. Once content teachers realize this, they will probably not feel that working on subject-specific language is an added extra for which they have no time but realize that doing this kind of work actually improves students' learning and understanding of the content subject itself (Beacco et al., 2015). I am currently supervising a PhD thesis of a history teacher who has incorporated literacy development into his everyday teaching, and, judging from the results of his research, by working on how the critical analysis of historical sources is structured and expressed, students not only improve their ability to write texts but also their skill in analysing sources, relating them to the historical period in which they were created and identifying and describing the debate surrounding them. This means that working on language actually improves students' cognitive performance (Meyer et al., 2015).

Outlook

In the next and final chapter, we are going to discuss some of the main difficulties faced by teachers when working with this approach and how they could be dealt with. We will also look at teacher training and why collaborative work is so important in this approach.

References

Beacco, J., Coste, D., Linneweber-Lammerskitten, H., Pieper, I., van de Ven, P., & Vollmer, H. J. (2015). *The place of the languages of schooling in the curricula.* https://www.ecml.at/Portals/1/documents/CoE-documents/Place-of-languages-of-schooling-in-curricula_EN.pdf

Bransford, J. D., Brown, A. L., & Cocking, R. D. (1999). *How people learn: Brain, mind, experience and school.* National Research Council.

Cenoz, J. (2015). Content-based instruction and content and language integrated learning: The same or different? *Language, Culture and Curriculum, 28*(1), 8–24.

Halbach, A. (2020). English language teaching goes CLIL: Fostering literacy and language development in secondary schools in Spain. In P. Mickan & I. Wallace (Eds.), *Handbook of language education curriculum design* (pp. 175–189). Routledge.

Madrid. (2018). *ORDEN 2876/2018, de 27 de julio, de la Consejería de Educación e Investigación, por la que se establece el currículo de inglés avanzado de Educación Secundaria Obligatoria en institutos y centros privados concertados bilingües español-inglés de la Comunidad de Madrid, y de Bachillerato, en institutos bilingües español-inglés de la Comunidad de Madrid.* BOCM 202, viernes 27 de agosto de 2018, 53–118.

Meyer, O., Coyle, D., Halbach, A., Schuck, K., & Ting, T. (2015). A pluriliteracies approach to content and language integrated learning—mapping learner progressions in knowledge construction and meaning-making. *Language, Culture, and Curriculum, 28*(1), 41–57. https://doi.org/10.1080/07908318.2014.1000924

Pellegrino, J. W., & Hilton, M. L. (2012). *Education for life and work.* National Academies Press. https://doi.org/10.17226/13398; https://www.nap.edu/catalog/13398/education-for-life-and-work-developing-transferable-knowledge-and-skills

CHAPTER 7

Teachers and the Literacy Approach

Abstract This final chapter looks at some of the main difficulties faced by teachers when working with the Literacy Approach. It also looks at teacher training and discusses what I have found to be the most important characteristics that make provisions for teacher training effective. The chapter finishes by looking at how, in our globalized world, language teaching has to change and why this change is best effected through a focus on literacy development.

JUST TAKE ANY STEP, WHETHER SMALL OR LARGE …

When we have a clear picture of what we want to happen and then things don't turn out as we hoped, the possibilities of getting frustrated—and sometimes even angry—are considerable. Over the years I have seen many teachers trying to work with literacy in their classroom, and often what I witnessed was not what I would have liked to see. However, little by little, I have come to acknowledge that change is very difficult and that what I am proposing through this Literacy Approach is so different from the way foreign or second languages are taught that it takes time to grow on practitioners. And yet, curiously enough, the most important difficulty for teachers to start making sense of the approach is precisely that they feel it is no different from what they are already doing.

To a certain extent, it is obvious that teachers should feel this way, as we all work with texts in our foreign language classes, we all do reading or listening exercises, and the tasks we propose are not much different from what we normally do in class. And yet, there is a fundamental difference in the aim of our teaching and this is that we are no longer interested in developing students' ability to communicate in the foreign language, but the focus is on communicating skilfully, using our understanding of how texts work to build up students' language skills—certainly—but also their text awareness, their feel for the language and their ability to create an effect in the reader/listener/viewer. This means that the communicative potential of the language is exploited to a completely different degree.

If we look at the way we work, another important difference lies in how the learning path gradually builds up students' skills and understandings to make them able to produce texts skilfully. By doing this, the planning of the unit takes into account where students are at the moment the unit is taught, identifies where they need to get in order to produce the required text and designs the teaching and learning tasks accordingly. It creates the conditions necessary for everyone to succeed. The teaching is therefore learner-centred and success-driven. Can we say the same about the approach we are currently using?

This leads us to the second difficulty: many teachers find it hard to identify the teaching points of a text, i.e., those characteristics that are worth looking at and that will make it possible for students to produce good texts themselves. This is something that also makes it difficult for teachers to give good feedback on students' production. Without a good understanding of the nature of the different types of texts or the characteristics of communication in different modes, and without a certain sensitivity towards the use of language or the way information is presented and arguments are constructed in a given text, it is very difficult to know what to focus on to make sure students are able to produce texts successfully. Working with a classification of text types with their corresponding typical features, as shown in Table 2.1, already goes some way in helping teachers with this task, but the awareness of how texts work only develops over time and with a lot of practice. This is something we need to keep in mind when we train teachers for this approach, especially since I am not aware of any initial teacher training that includes a focus on text awareness raising.

The identification of the teaching points in a text is further complicated by the fact that, in many contexts, teachers feel a lot of pressure to cover the curriculum. I have seen teachers include the position of adverbs among the teaching points for a model text that does not use any adverbs at all. These teachers were clearly trying to accommodate the curriculum rather than looking at what the model text had to offer. As teachers become more confident in using the curriculum as a guide rather than a detailed schedule laying down what needs to be taught when, and as they develop their own text awareness, it should become easier for them to identify the teaching points and match them with the curriculum. The key is probably to look at the text with open eyes and curiosity and allow oneself to be surprised, intrigued or excited by its textual qualities, as well as by its content and meaning. Starting from this excitement, teachers can then try to identify the features that are responsible for creating it and, by doing so, identify the elements that are worth teaching.

Related to the teaching points is a further difficulty. Sometimes teachers do good work on the model text, but they forget about the production aim or choose a production aim that is related with the content of the text or its topic rather than with the text type exemplified by the model text. While, of course, using the first text as an "inspiration" in terms of content for students' production of a new text type that responds to the input text is possible, students will still need to work on the text type they are required to produce. Students need models to guide their own text production. This means that if I read a passage from one of the Harry Potter books and I want my students to write a characterization of one of the characters, I need to give them a model of this text type, i.e., a model characterization to which they can look for support. The input text is a narrative that gives the students the content to write about, but the model text that will help them in their production has to be a characterization, i.e. a descriptive text.

However, it sometimes also happens that teachers simply do not work towards a production aim. This is quite frequent in primary education, where teachers feel that students are not able to produce their own texts. However, if the learning path is well constructed and offers students the support they need, even young students with a low level in the foreign language are able to produce text. Beyond these considerations about the difficulty of the task being balanced by the support given, the fact that the final production aim is omitted leaves the work done in the unit without a purpose. What is powerful in this approach is the fact that the textual features and linguistic elements the students work on are immediately relevant to their own production, which makes this work both meaningful and useful. Students remember what they learn through the Literacy Approach, they remember text models and language, because they were useful.

> When the children needed to talk about people who share certain characteristics, they hummed the song to remember a good model to create a description. (Marta, primary teacher)

A final difficulty that I have found teachers have is related to the design of the learning path. To be honest, this is a difficulty that I found quite baffling, but that probably shows how much teachers in my context rely uncritically on textbooks for their teaching and how little they are used to focusing on the process of teaching. I find that teachers often construct a learning path that contains activities that are not linked in any clear way to each other and that do not contribute to building up students' understanding and skills so that they are able to produce a text successfully. For me it is as if they were not able to imagine or visualize the work they are planning, and this sometimes means that they ask students to do things they haven't taught them to do. Maybe we need to use more imagination for this visualization, but maybe this difficulty is simply the reflection of all the challenges mentioned above: if I feel the Literacy Approach is not much of a novelty, I am not able to identify the teaching points a text offers or I forget about the production aim, then constructing a coherent learning path becomes something of an impossibility.

Does it surprise you, then, that I sometimes get frustrated in the light of these difficulties? And yet, over the years I have understood that often the change proposed through the Literacy Approach starts very small, not by using the approach from A to Z but maybe by working on a text that is not in the textbook or by scaffolding students' production more carefully. Once teachers have started using texts rather than textbooks, working towards a production aim or looking at how a text works, these partial changes develop their own dynamics, making teachers question their practices, opening their eyes to different ways of understanding language teaching and increasing their motivation. They start asking questions, introduce more small changes and, if given the possibility of confronting what they do with the original ideas in the Literacy Approach, develop a deeper understanding of what it entails. But this takes time, and the result does not always fully match my own understanding of the Literacy Approach.

But this is not all: the way some practitioners have struggled with the Literacy Approach, the challenges they faced to make sense of it, has also allowed me to refine, think again, question, discuss and develop the initial ideas about the approach, and the result of this process of "interthinking" (Littleton & Mercer, 2013) is what you now hold in your hands. I trust—and do hope—that this is not the end of this process of developing a new approach to foreign language teaching through a focus on literacy that already spans at least five years. The approach still needs to prove its worth in some contexts and much more data is necessary to really allow me to claim its proven worth. What we have so far is some scientific evidence (Jechimer, 2022) and a lot of experience that allows us to claim its usefulness.

Training the Teachers

As with any approach, methodology or teaching innovation, it is the teachers who ultimately transfer it into the real world by putting it into practice. However, as should have become apparent in the section above, this does not happen spontaneously and is even less a change that can be effected immediately. Rather, it takes time, training and experimentation. Over the years I have had many opportunities to train different groups of teachers in using this approach, both pre-service and in-service, through short courses or longer, and in the past year and a half increasingly online rather than face to face. There are three characteristics of these training opportunities that I feel have determined the extent to which the training provisions were successful, and they are related to the possibility of experiencing what it means to work with the approach, the opportunity to work over a longer period of time in a process to refine one's understanding of the approach and finally the possibility to put it into practice.

As far as the possibility of experiencing the approach is concerned, I have often found that when the approach is first explained, teachers feel that it is very similar to what they are already doing. Even showing them video recordings of classes that use this approach (e.g. from https://repository.lit4clil.uw.edu.pl/#) is often not enough to make trainees understand how the approach works. However, in my experience, teaching them a short literacy unit suddenly changes their perception. It is as if feeling the difference paves the way to understanding it—which doesn't mean, however, that this understanding emerges suddenly as a result of the experience. Rather, to start coming to terms with how the Literacy

Approach works, trainees need to get down to the practice and create units of work, hopefully together with other practitioners, so that the discussions that emerge along the way help them build a sounder understanding of the approach. If this work is carefully guided and supported by a trainer, and participants have the opportunity to engage in this process of collectively making sense of the approach, understanding is likely to grow over time.

However, the final test is going to come from the practice, when teachers implement the units and observe the students' reactions to it, their learning and the effect of the way of working on students' motivation as well as on their own as teachers. Often, when they first engage in teaching a unit of this kind, teachers are not fully aware of its implications, and it is only when they see how it affects their students that they realize to what extent this way of learning makes a difference. Most of the teachers I have been able to accompany through this process of implementation are surprised by it but also feel that working in this way challenges their beliefs and prior way of teaching. This, again, raises questions which have the potential to make teachers develop a deeper understanding of what is at stake, provided they have somebody with whom they can talk about the approach or some other way of contrasting what they are doing and seeing with the ideas behind the Literacy Approach.

I find this methodology extremely motivating both for teachers and for students. (Fiona, primary teacher)

In this sense, by far the most impactful training opportunities I have participated in so far have been an Erasmus+ project in which teachers from three countries created and implemented the literacy units you can find at https://repository.lit4clil.uw.edu.pl/# and the process of supervising a teacher's MA thesis—and then PhD thesis—about the Literacy Approach. Both were long-term projects with a direct link to classroom practice, and both included many opportunities to share emerging understanding and questions with fellow teachers and trainers. And yet, as I mentioned in the previous section, not all participants were able to build their understanding in the same way nor were they able to make sense of the approach to the same extent. However, the process that was initiated through these two training opportunities is ongoing, and I am sure that for all participating teachers it constitutes a huge opportunity for growth.

Why Literacy, Why Now?

A few decades ago, it was language teachers who opened the door not only to learning and communicating in a foreign language for many students but also to developing intercultural skills and learning about the target culture. Students depended on their teachers as good models of language use and as sources of input in the target language. This has changed drastically. Nowadays, we have almost unlimited access to foreign languages through the Internet. Our students play videogames with speakers of different languages, listen to music in a foreign language, are able to watch series and films in almost any language of their choice, and when they want to understand a bit more about how the language works, they can look for video tutorials by expert teachers—many of whom are much more fun to watch than we are. They can also use apps to learn the language, read simplified texts online or listen to podcasts especially prepared for foreign language students. The wealth of materials is, of course, much greater for some languages than others, but I doubt there are many languages that are not present on the Internet in some way or other—one of my sons is currently learning Swahili with the help of some video tutorials.

Conversely, students do not need to speak "a bit" of the foreign language; rather, in order to fully participate in our globalized world, they need to be literate in several languages. Not only will they have to work in international teams, access knowledge in different languages and live in different parts of the world for shorter or longer periods of time in the future, but many of them are already using different languages at school, either because they are learning part of their content subject in a foreign language, because the material used in class is written in a foreign language or because the language of schooling is not their mother tongue. For all of them, the foreign language is a tool for academic success, a gateway to participate in society, rather than an object of study.

Both the presence of foreign languages in our everyday world and the increased need to be able to use it skilfully for learning change the role of the teacher. We are no longer that necessary as providers of input or even explanation. We are no longer needed as the only models of good language use either. What we are necessary for is, as we said in Chap. 1, to make sure students develop their ability to "acquir[e], create, connect and communicat[e] meaning in a wide variety of contexts" (Government of Alberta, 2009), through a variety of languages. By doing so we have the possibility of engaging students in cognitively challenging work that contributes to developing their thinking skills and learning strategies. This is what literacy-based language teaching has to offer.

Finally, as was argued at the beginning of this book, working on literacy development will contribute to foster the development of the skills that will allow students to fully participate in academia first and, by extension, in society in general. This literacy development could thus be planned for across the languages in the curriculum, allowing for transfer between language subjects and incorporating all the other languages the students bring into school, in what Lyster (2015) has called a "cross-lingual pedagogy". In our world, characterized by migration and globalization,

> we can no longer think of homogeneous classes of students who have the majority language as their L1 [...] In the twenty-first century [...] programs will increasingly have students of majority, minority and immigrant languages in the same class. These students are very often multilingual speakers with different languages in their linguistic repertoire. The need to develop metalinguistic and language awareness taking the students' own repertoire as the point of departure creates the need [...] to adopt a multilingual focus so as to integrate not only language and content but also all the languages in students' multilingual repertoires. (Cenoz, 2015, p. 22)

Shifting the focus of foreign language teaching to literacy development makes such a multilingual approach possible.

REFERENCES

Cenoz, J. (2015). Content-based instruction and content and language integrated learning: The same or different? *Language, Culture and Curriculum, 28*(1), 8–24.

Government of Alberta. (2009). *Living literacy: A literacy framework for Alberta's next generation economy*. Alberta Advanced Education and Technology. https://deslibris.ca/ID/220887

Jechimer, E. (2022). *The literacy approach to improve EFL learning in primary education in CLIL contexts: An evaluation study*. Doctoral dissertation, University of Alcalá.

Littleton, K., & Mercer, N. (2013). *Interthinking: Putting talk to work*. Routledge.

Lyster, R. (2015). Using form-focused tasks to integrate language across the immersion curriculum. *System, 54*, 4–13. https://doi.org/10.1016/j.system.2014.09.022

Appendix A: Tasks for the Reception Phase of a Unit Based on *We Were Liars* by E. Lockhart

Pre-reading

Think about your family for a minute, take some notes about what is important for them, how they behave, etc. Describe your family to your partner and let him or her ask questions.

Reading

1. You are now going to read Chap. 1 of a novel by E. Lockhart called *We Were Liars*.[1] It contains a description of a family. What is your first reaction?
2. Our first reaction is probably bafflement. Who is this family? Why are there contradictions?

   Can you try to describe this family? What tells you that this is the way they are?

   In the text, there are negative descriptions. Do you think they mean what they say?

---

[1] Despite my best efforts, I was unable to secure permission from the publishers to reproduce the text here. It is, however, available on the Internet.

Do an Internet search for the cover of the book. Does this cover help you answer the previous question? Does it give you any information about the novel itself? Does the writing tell a further story?

3. We are now going to look at the description in greater detail. It is clear that one thing is what the text says, another what it means. In pairs, fill in the following table with the negative statements about the Sinclairs which describe what they are not and what doesn't matter. Then think about what this is probably saying, and finally, when you have interpreted all the negative statements, try to find an adjective that describes the Sinclairs:

THE SINCLAIRS: A _____ FAMILY

What the text says	What it means
No one is a criminal	
It doesn't matter if divorce shreds …	

The Sinclairs are also described in relation to their physical appearance. Again, these physical characteristics have a meaning beyond what they describe:

The Sinclairs, a Beautiful Family

Physical appearance	What it means
Tall, athletic, handsome	
Old-money Democrats	

So who are the Sinclairs? What are they like?

In the tables above you have recorded different sentences that express something different from what they say. How does this work? Can you describe the strategies the author uses to create this effect?

Appendix B: Checklist of Contents for Year 10 in the Curriculum of Advanced English (Comunidad de Madrid, Spain)

	Covered in the unit
Listening	
Classroom interaction with teachers and peers	
Predicting the content of reports, documentaries, debates and speeches	
General understanding of both formal and spontaneous reports, speeches and debates	
Understanding of summaries of data and research about a known topic	
Understanding of reports, TV programmes and films both in standard and non-standard English when the image supports understanding	
Identification of the speaker's intention: clarifying an idea, guiding the listener through rhetoric questions, use of irony, etc.	
Distinguishing between facts and opinions in both formal and spontaneous debates and presentations	
Evaluation of the objectivity in the presentation of ideas, description of events, etc.	
Inference of points of view that are not overtly expressed	
Distinguishing between main ideas, justifications and examples in debates and well-structured presentations both in standard and non-standard English about a known topic	

(*continued*)

(continued)

	Covered in the unit
Ability to follow a fast, spontaneous conversation well enough to be able to take part in it	
Understanding specific information in presentations, conversations and linguistically complex debates about a known topic	
Identifying the speaker's intention and feelings using linguistic (choice of lexis and syntactic structures) or paralinguistic features (rhythm, accent, body language)	
Ability to identify and analyse the role of the fictional elements (setting, characters and narrative time) in films	
Ability to understand the message despite the presence of unknown vocabulary, problems in the recording or background noise	
Speaking	
Participation in daily interaction in the classroom, especially in pair and group work as well as in interaction with the teacher	
Participation in discussions: presenting one's own opinions accurately, refuting the opinions of others, asking for clarification, asking questions, etc.	
Production of detailed, clearly structured and prepared presentations on topics or issues of interest to them in different formats (reports, speeches, presentations)	
Ability to structure a presentation or intervention in a debate in a coherent and convincing way, distinguishing between main and secondary ideas, using examples and stylistic elements (irony, exaggeration, personification, rhetorical question, etc.) to give force to the points of view and arguments used	
Ability to deviate from the prepared script in discussions and presentations to respond to interventions of other participants or requests for clarification	
Ability to initiate, maintain and complete conversations in more or less formal contexts and to repair problems that may arise through repetition, paraphrasing or clarification	
Ability to respond to questions and requests for clarification or repetition and correct errors if they have led to confusion	
Effective use of connectors typical of spoken language to identify the relationship between ideas	
Ability to differentiate between a more or less formal register and choose the most appropriate one for each communicative situation	
Ability to describe and explain a graph or illustration to support an argument	
Ability to summarize what has been heard by way of clarification	
Ability to use synonyms, approximations and paraphrases in situations where he or she does not know a particular term	

(*continued*)

(continued)

	Covered in the unit
Ability to express attitudes and points of view indirectly	
Ability to gather and select relevant information from different sources and summarize it for presentation purposes	
Effective use of ICT resources for oral presentations in different modalities (visual, audio-visual, digital)	
Pronunciation, accentuation, intonation and rhythm without errors that could lead to confusion	
Reading	
Anticipation of content in literary, argumentative and opinion texts with different levels of formality	
Ability to adapt reading strategy to the characteristics of the text and the needs of the task (skimming, scanning, extensive reading, intensive reading)	
General and detailed comprehension of literary, argumentative and opinion texts with varying levels of formality	
Differentiation between main ideas and justifications and examples in argumentative and opinion texts	
Ability to identify the author's intention and points of view from linguistic parameters (choice of lexis and syntactic structures)	
Understanding the effect and meaning of stylistic elements and discursive strategies in literary and non-literary texts (irony, metaphor, personification, generalization, etc.)	
Comprehension of the text despite the presence of unfamiliar vocabulary	
Ability to identify and analyse the role of fictional elements (location, characters and narrative) in literary texts of different genres (narrative, poetry and drama)	
Ability to identify when an author is using others' ideas (paraphrasing or quoting), and when the ideas are their own	
Critical ability to evaluate the quality of a text in terms of argumentation, objectivity, effectiveness and quality of sources used	
Inference of points of view and opinions which are not expressed openly	
Identifying the organizing principles that structure a text	
Supporting interpretations of the meaning, effect or quality of a text with evidence taken from the text	
Writing	
Production of formal and informal argumentative and opinion texts with the help of models	
Ability to express the same idea using different registers	

(*continued*)

(continued)

	Covered in the unit
Use of different levels of abstraction in different parts of the text	
Ability to describe and explain a graph, table or illustration as part of an informative text	
Ability to combine different sub-genres in the same text (summary, description, critical commentary, etc.)	
Ability to express and describe a problem or fact with a certain degree of detail	
Ability to construct coherent arguments with a clear logical structure	
Ability to express the result of a literary analysis identifying and analysing the role of fictional elements (location, characters and narrative) in literary texts of different genres (narrative, poetry and drama)	
Elaboration of the main ideas in an argumentative and expository text by means of examples, explanations and justifications	
Use of evidence to strengthen the argument (evidence from the commented text, data, statistics, etc.) in such a way that they are integrated in the written text	
Ability to collect, select and synthesize information from different sources and summarize it	
Use of organizational principles to structure the written text effectively, also in the case of a longer text	
Use of elements to ensure coherence and cohesion of texts (connectors, correct use of references, synonyms, etc.)	
Use of a variety of sentence structures to maintain the reader's interest	
Ability to divide the text into paragraphs with a clear structure, and to write a clearly structured introduction (thesis statement) and a conclusion which closes the text in a convincing way	
Ability to generate ideas and search for information, plan the structure of the text, identify the necessary linguistic resources, etc.	
Iterative drafting of texts in which parts are written, read, modified, rewritten, etc.	
Language functions: use of the following linguistic functions at an intermediate-advanced level, both orally and in writing	
Describe: *There is/there are …; The first impression we get of X is …; Its main characteristic is …*	
Define: *X is a Y that …*	
Summarize: *This text/film is about …; On the whole, the text is saying …; In this text the author is saying …; In this text the author indicates/points out/emphasizes/concludes that …: To support the main claim, the author provides evidence that …*	

(*continued*)

(continued)

	Covered in the unit
Construct understanding building on other people's: *My idea/explanation is similar to/related to …*; *My idea builds upon X's idea that …*; *I agree but would phrase it a bit differently/add something else/look at it from a different perspective*	
Justify: *The reason is …*; *This can be seen from …*; *I believe this because …*; *My primary reason for thinking so is …*; *Perhaps the most convincing reason for thinking so is …*	
Give opinions, rebut: *Based on my experience, I think/believe that …*; *In my opinion …*; *As for me …*; *I don't agree …*; *I see your point, but …*; *Unlike X, I think/believe that …*; *I see it differently*	
Asking for opinions: *What do you think? Do you agree? What about you? What do you make of this? What is your take on X?*	
Asking for information/clarification: *Something else I'd like to know …*; *Could you be more specific about this? If I have understood correctly, your point is that …*; *Sorry, but I'm not (quite) clear on …*; *In other words, you think …*	
Paraphrase: *So you are saying that …*; *What I hear you saying is that …*; *In other words, you think …*	
Give information: *The statistics are misleading because they do (not) show …*; *These facts/reasons/data strongly suggest that …*; *Yet some authors maintain that …*	
Expressing cause and effect: *The most likely reason for X was Y*; *X wasn't caused by Y because …*; *Several factors led to the outcome. First, …*; *The change resulted in …*; *The X led to Y, which in turn led to Z*	
Analyse: *We can interpret X as …*; *Given the evidence, we can deduce that …*; *X is related to Y in so far as …*; *We can draw parallels between texts/characters/the setting and the narrative because …*	
Present interpretations tentatively: *X seems to indicate that …*; *X could be interpreted as meaning …*; *We could assume X to mean …*; *This would mean that …*	
Present arguments: *Based on the evidence presented so far, I believe that …*; *The advantages of … outweigh the disadvantages of … insofar as ….*; *Although some people claim that …, opponents argue that ….*	
Finish argumentations: *At the end of the day …*; *Summing up …*; *Having reached this point …*	
Grammatical structures	
Idiomatic expressions of time: *on the brink of/on the point of*	
Complex conditional structures: *should*, *only if*, and *as if/as though*	

(*continued*)

(continued)

	Covered in the unit
Academic register characterized by passive constructions (*It is generally believed that ...*), nominalizations (*the development of the main character*), complex attributive constructions (*the narrative tension created by the author in this text*) and technical vocabulary (*personification*)	
Complex relative clauses; relative clauses with prepositions: *In the churchyard there is a huge stone, from which the village takes its name/... which the village takes its name from*	
Clefting and fronting for emphasis: *Under no circumstances should you talk to strangers; No matter what she says, they always laugh*	
Reduced adverbial clauses (*Having had a similar experience earlier, he knew exactly how to act*)	
Complex passive constructions (*My parrot loves to be talked to; It could be achieved; This needs to be done; It was thought that/it was assumed that ...; Children love being read to; The houses had already been destroyed; This needs to be given some attention*)	
Lexis	
Use of common expressions, lexis and fixed phrases about topics of general and personal interest, everyday topics or contents of other subjects in the curriculum	
Recognizing synonyms, antonyms and *"false friends"*	
Use of a variety of linkers: *due to; so; though; unless; so as; in order not to; however; on condition that ...*	
Use of common academic vocabulary according to the *Academic Word List*, such as *authority; available; benefit; constitutional; economic; established; evidence; identified; legal; legislation; major; policy; principle; procedure; research; significant; similar; source; specific; structure; theory*	
Understanding common academic vocabulary according to the *Academic Word List*, such as: *achieve; affect; appropriate; aspects; categories; chapter; complex; conclusion; consequences; cultural; design; elements; evaluation; features; final; focus; impact; items; obtained; perceived; positive; potential; previous; primary; region; relevant; resources; restricted; sought; select; strategies; survey; text; traditional; transfer*	
Pronunciation	
Using appropriate rhythm, intonation, sentence and word stress	
Correct pronunciation of the sounds of English: fricative and affricate consonants: /θ/, /ð/, /ʃ/, /ʒ/, /dʒ/, /tʃ/	
Recognizing phonetic symbols	

Adapted from http://www.bocm.es/boletin/CM_Orden_BOCM/2018/08/24/BOCM-20180824-12.PDF

Index

A
Analysing, 22, 23, 25, 33, 36, 46, 57, 64, 70
Assessment, 57
  formative, 57
  as learning, 57
  self-, 58

B
Backward design, 14, 15, 74
Backward planning, 18, 19, 23

C
Content and Language Integrated Learning (CLIL), 2, 82, 84
Curriculum, 2, 13, 27, 72–74, 77–79, 83, 84, 87, 91, 96

F
Free production, 23, 46, 47, 50, 51

G
Guided production, 22, 23, 46, 47, 49, 57

L
Learning path, 19–23, 29–31, 34, 37–44, 51, 56, 57, 63, 64, 70, 84, 90–92
Literacy, 3–7, 23, 63, 77, 82, 87, 89, 93, 95–96

O
Observing, 22, 23, 33, 34, 46, 50, 57, 64, 70, 71

P

Planning grid, 23, 26, 29, 36–38, 41, 47, 57, 61, 63, 70, 71, 74, 86

S

Scaffolding, 30, 31, 46, 54, 57, 64, 79, 92

T

Teaching points, 19, 23, 26, 29, 36–38, 41, 47, 51, 56, 61, 63, 70, 77, 84, 86, 90–92

Text type, 6, 7, 15, 18–20, 23, 30, 34, 36, 37, 52, 56, 61, 63, 74, 78, 79, 83, 84, 87, 91

Training, 94
   teacher, 90, 93, 94

Ingram Content Group UK Ltd.
Milton Keynes UK
UKHW020146050723
424579UK00004B/260